UNDERGROUND TRAIN FILE

TUBE STOCK 1933–1959

Brian Hardy

Capital Transport

AUTHOR'S NOTE AND INTRODUCTION

This handbook covers the period from 1933 to 1959 and contains complete listings of all London Transport Tube Stock passenger rail vehicles in stock during that period and gives a description of each type. The first date was chosen because the London Passenger Transport Board came into being on 1 July of that year.

Vehicles which were new during the period under review, and similarly those which were withdrawn and scrapped, are noted with the relevant dates alongside the appropriate cars. Previous numbers and cars involved in renumbering and conversions are also included. Quite often, the dates quoted will be 'official' dates, which may often be at variance with what actually happened – in some cases the dates may be a 'week-ending', or just a month and year.

Prior to 1933, transport in London had been operated by a number of different companies and the new LPTB embraced those who operated Underground railways, buses and trams. Insofar as the Underground was concerned, it was a case of the Metropolitan Railway joining up with what had become the Underground Electric Railways of London (UERL), which comprised what we now know as the District, Bakerloo, Central, Piccadilly and Northern lines.

The story then takes us through the Second World War. This in itself is most interesting, in as much as new rolling stock was being delivered but many of the older cars, which were destined for service on other and extended lines, ended up being stored, as were many cars that would normally have been scrapped – they were kept as spare vehicles, 'just in case'.

After the Second World War, there was much re-appraisal of the pre-war plans, which had a significant effect on rolling stock. The austere post-war conditions meant that any proposed new rolling stock came under intensive scrutiny and although work on the Central Line extensions resumed, those for the Northern Line were put on the back burner and subsequently abandoned, as were those for the extension of the Bakerloo Line to Camberwell Green.

This publication would not have been possible without the kind help of Dr Andrew Gilks, who spent many hours meticulously recording the disposal details of the older rolling stock types, J. Graeme Bruce OBE, who was involved with LT rolling stock for all of his working life and to Piers Connor who kept immaculate records on London Transport railway rolling stock. And, of course, to London Transport, whose decision to run down the Car Records office at Acton Works in the late-1970s enabled the rescue of many historical records and data, which would otherwise have been consigned to the dustbin. My thanks also go to my wife Jeanne, for her help with the typescript and checking of the numerical data.

Overleaf The Piccadilly Line reached Hounslow West in March 1933, where a two-car train of Pre-1938 Tube Stock is seen in the middle platform. It should be noted that the leading car, a 1928 UCC control trailer, was one of four that were fitted with automatic couplers as an experiment. On the basis that two of the cars that took part in the experiment were on the Piccadilly Line (the other two were on the Bakerloo), this must have been either 5012 or 5046. *Charles F. Klapper/LURS*

CONTENTS

First published 2001
ISBN 185414 235 6
Published by Capital Transport Publishing, 38 Long Elmes, Harrow Weald, Middlesex
Printed by CS Graphics, Singapore

CHAPTER ONE

CENTRAL LONDON RAILWAY 1903 STOCK

The Central London Railway passenger fleet inherited by the LPTB in 1933 comprised 259 cars, consisting of 88 motor cars, 99 trailers and 72 control trailers. Of the 171 trailers and control trailers, 165 of them dated back to when the line opened in 1900 and had been built as locomotive-hauled carriages.

The unsatisfactory performance of the electric locomotives at that time, primarily because of the vibration to property above as a result of their unsprung weight, led to them being replaced in 1903 by multiple-unit motor coaches, following trials with four such cars converted from trailers. The result was 64 motors built by MAR (24 cars) and BRCW (40 cars). These, along with the original trailers, were provided with hand-operated gates at the car ends. The original trailers of 1900/01 comprised 143 from Ashbury (1–125 and 151–168) and 25 from Brush (126–150). Along with the new motor coaches of 1903, there were six new trailers from BRCW, four replacing those converted as motor car prototypes (54, 81, 84 and 88) and two being additional stock (169–170). The last locomotive-hauled train operated on the CLR on 8 June 1903. Two of the motor car prototypes were reconverted to trailers in 1906, taking the new numbers 171–172, whilst the other two were retained as battery locomotives.

A 1903-built driving motor car leads a three-coach short train at the new Central London station at Holborn, which opened in September 1933 to provide better interchange with the Piccadilly Line. Note the CLR's third rail current system, which remained in use until May 1940. *LT Museum*

A 1917 Brush-built motor car leads a three-car train on the approach to Ealing Broadway, before renumbering into the 39xx series, which was done to all the stock between 1933 and 1935. All but two of these motor cars started life on loan to the Bakerloo for the Watford extension and worked on that line from 1917 to 1920. *Author's collection*

To operate short trains in off-peak times, a programme began in 1908 to convert some trailers to control trailers. The first 28 cars comprised 14 'A' end and 14 'B' end from the 1900 Brush-built batch (22 cars) and all six of the 1903 BRCW cars. These were provided with roller shutters at the cab ends, whereas subsequent conversions had standard end cab doors. One control trailer car, No. 102, was scrapped in 1913 as a result of a collision at Shepherd's Bush. It was replaced when more control trailer conversions were undertaken, but the fleet remained one car short.

The fleet was augmented in 1920 with new motor coaches built by Brush, for the extension to Ealing Broadway. The First World War, however, delayed the completion of the work. The cars, being built by 1917, first saw service (with spare 'Gate' stock trailers from the Piccadilly Line) on the Bakerloo extension to Watford Junction, whose rolling stock deliveries were delayed for the same reason. Some of the 1900/01 trailers and control trailers were modified to run with the new motor cars and were given the title of 'Ealing' stock. The 22 CTs known as Ealing stock were converted in 1915 and stored at Wood Lane depot until required for the CLR. The older cars meanwhile became known as 'Tunnel' stock, and being unsuitable for open air running, were mostly confined to the Wood Lane to Liverpool Street service. There were thus two distinct types of rolling stock.

As with the 'Gate' tube stock on the Bakerloo, Piccadilly and Hampstead, the question of stock replacement or modernisation had to be considered. For the three tube lines financed by C. T. Yerkes, which opened in 1906–07, new stock was chosen, but for Central London it was decided to convert the cars to air door operation, for a further ten years or so additional life. The decision was based on the fact that the Central London cars had wooden bodies which were easier to convert than the steel bodies of the LER cars. A prototype conversion was undertaken on trailer car 40 in 1925 and operated as part of a normal train, the air doors being controlled by the gateman. Following its success, the conversion work on the remainder of the fleet was undertaken by the Union Construction and Finance Co. at Feltham, to where the cars were taken by road. At this time the cars were renumbered by the LER in 1926–27 (motor cars 392–479, trailers 955–1053 and control trailers 1849–1920). Trailers and control trailers had two pairs of double doors per side while motor cars had one. For the first time control trailers were separated from the passenger saloon and were fully enclosed. The cabs of driving motor cars were anyway separated from the public by the equipment compartment immediately behind. The first complete air-door train of CLR stock entered service in September 1926. To enhance the Ealing service an additional eight motor cars and eight control trailers were converted from the 1903 fleet and were known as 'Ealing Stock – Yorke conversions' after the name of the then Line Superintendent C. T. Yorke, who ordered the work to be undertaken.

During part of the conversion period, two six-car trains of 1920 air-door stock (with converted 'French' motor cars) were loaned to the Central London from the Piccadilly. In fact the CLR stock was to continue in service for another 12 years

Interior of a CLR trailer car, after conversion to air doors. Much was done to make these trains comparable to the Pre-1938 Tube Stock then being introduced on other lines.
LT Museum

or so, all cars being renumbered in 1933–34 to 39xx (motors), 59xx (control trailers) and 79xx (trailers). Under the 1935–40 New Works programme, which was to include extensions to the Central Line at both east and west ends, the 1903–20 trains were replaced by the Pre-1938 type transferred from the Northern Line, the first of these running in the autumn of 1938 on the CLR's 3rd (centre) rail system. The last of the old trains ran in normal passenger service on 10 June 1939 and although some were scrapped, many were retained. A total of 36 'Tunnel' motor coaches were converted into double-ended sleet locomotives in 1939–40 (numbered ESL100–117) for winter de-icing, whilst two 'Ealing' motor cars were converted into a double-ended diesel-electric locomotive (DEL120) in 1941. Although one sleet locomotive was scrapped because of collision damage in 1953, the other 17 remained active at the end of 1959.

Operational experience with the diesel-electric locomotive conversion was not as successful as it was hoped, mainly because of sighting difficulties for drivers, and plans for other conversions were abandoned. In its last few years of service, it operated solely as an electric locomotive. With the conversion of both sleet and diesel locomotives, the work involved cutting off the passenger saloon and joining the trailing ends of them to form a double-ended locomotive. Insofar as the sleet locomotives were concerned, in addition to the motor bogies at each end, a pair of bogies were added between the centre section which carried the de-icing gear. De-icing fluid was fed to the equipment from tanks under the centre section of the car. The first conversion, ESL100 had only one bogie in the centre but was soon modified, the other locomotives following the latter design. The slight differences with ESL100 continued to identify it as the 'prototype' conversion.

After the outbreak of the Second World War, the Government decided that no withdrawn rolling stock should be scrapped. Therefore, those CLR cars not already scrapped were retained in case of extensive damage to rolling stock through enemy action, some being stored at the partially completed Ruislip depot, with the possibility of them being made available for service, should the need arise. Because the old CLR centre 3rd-rail system had been done away with, the likelihood of using these cars again was nil and thus the decision was taken for the majority of them to be scrapped, much of which was done during 1942–43. Four 1903 motor cars (3946, 3973, 3977 and 3988) were retained, the latter pair for pilot duties for the forthcoming five-car Instruction train. In the end, it was decided that the work could be done by existing ballast motor cars and all four remaining cars were scrapped in 1948–49.

CENTRAL LONDON STOCK SUMMARY – DISPOSAL OF CARS

End-Year	'Tunnel' Stock			'Ealing' Stock			Ealing/Yorke		Scrapped	Total Scrapped	Stock Remaining
	DM	T	CT	DM	T	CT	DM	CT			
Stock inherited 1 July 1933:											
	56	75	40	24	24	24	8	8	–	–	259
1938	4	18	1	–	–	–	–	–	23	23	236
1939	34	27	14	6	14	13	7	4	119	142	117
1940	8	18	17	–	4	7	1	2	57	199	60
1942	6	11	8	18	6	4	–	2	55	254	5
1943	–	1	–	–	–	–	–	–	1	255	4
1948	2	–	–	–	–	–	–	–	2	257	2
1949	2	–	–	–	–	–	–	–	2	259	–
Total:	**56**	**75**	**40**	**24**	**24**	**24**	**8**	**8**	**259**	**259**	**–**

It should be noted that the disposal figures include those converted for Sleet/Diesel locomotives – the passenger saloons were scrapped but the motor car ends and equipment compartments were retained.

DRIVING MOTOR CARS

"EALING" STOCK
BUILT BY BRUSH 1915 – Total 24

CLR No.	B'loo No. (1917–20)	Reno (1926–28)	1930s No.	Disposal Date	CLR No.	B'loo No. (1917–20)	Reno (1926–28)	1930s No.	Disposal Date
269	291	392	**3912**	21.10.42	281	281	404	**3924**	09.10.39
270	294	393	**3913**	09.09.42	282	282	405	**3925**	26.10.42
271	293	394	**3914**	29.04.39	283	283	406	**3926**	13.07.42
272	–	395	**3915**	13.07.42	284	284	407	**3927**	13.07.42
273	273	396	**3916**	09.09.42	285	285	408	**3928**	13.07.42
274	274	397	**3917**	13.07.42	286	286	409	**3929**	09.09.42
275	275	398	**3918**	13.07.42	287	287	410	**3930**	10.02.39
276	276	399	**3919**	09.09.42	288	288	411	**3931**	15.06.42
277	277	400	**3920**	09.09.42	289	289	412	**3932**	10.11.39
278	278	401	**3921**	15.06.42	290	290	413	**3933**	10.02.39
279	279	402	**3922**	27.06.42	291	–	414	**3934**	21.10.42
280	280	403	**3923**	10.02.39	292	292	415	**3935**	09.09.42

Note * Cars 272 and 291 never worked on the Bakerloo Line.

"EALING" STOCK – YORKE CONVERSIONS
Built by MAR 1903 and converted in 1925 – Total 8

CLR No.	"Ealing" No.	Reno 1926–28	1930s No.	Disposal Date	CLR No.	"Ealing" No.	Reno 1926–28	1930s No.	Disposal Date
205	293	416	**3936**	28.02.40	206	297	420	**3940**	31.07.39
226	294	417	**3937**	31.07.39*	212	298	421	**3941**	31.07.39*
213	295	418	**3938**	31.07.39	227	299	422	**3942**	04.09.39
211	296	419	**3939**	04.09.39	220	300	423	**3943**	04.09.39

Note * Converted to diesel electric locomotive – date shown is scrapping of saloon section of car.

"TUNNEL" STOCK – Built by MAR 1903 – Total 16

CLR No.	Reno 1926–28	1930s No.	Disposal Date	CLR No.	Reno 1926–28	1930s No.	Disposal Date
208	424	**3944**	28.08.39*	219	432	**3952**	18.07.39*
207	425	**3945**	30.11.39*	218	433	**3953**	27.03.40*
210	426	**3946**	09.03.48	223	434	**3954**	09.04.40*
209	427	**3947**	12.12.38	221	435	**3955**	10.01.39
214	428	**3948**	03.06.42	224	436	**3956**	14.11.39*
215	429	**3949**	03.06.42	222	437	**3957**	03.06.42
217	430	**3950**	30.11.39*	225	438	**3958**	29.04.39*
216	431	**3951**	03.06.42	228	439	**3959**	14.11.39*

Note * Converted to sleet locomotive – date shown is scrapping of saloon section of car.

"TUNNEL" STOCK – Built by BRCW 1903 – Total 40

CLR No.	Reno 1926–28	1930s No.	Disposal Date	CLR No.	Reno 1926–28	1930s No.	Disposal Date
229	440	**3960**	17.11.38*	242	451	**3971**	28.06.39*
231	441	**3961**	19.01.39	241	452	**3972**	28.09.39*
230	442	**3962**	18.12.39*	243	453	**3973**	26.03.48
233	443	**3963**	28.09.39	245	454	**3974**	10.01.39
234	444	**3964**	27.03.40*	244	455	**3975**	03.01.39
236	445	**3965**	28.06.39*	246	456	**3976**	28.06.39*
235	446	**3966**	31.01.39	248	457	**3977**	03.05.49
238	447	**3967**	09.02.40*	247	458	**3978**	12.12.38
237	448	**3968**	19.01.39*	249	459	**3979**	28.06.39*
240	449	**3969**	18.12.39*	250	460	**3980**	28.06.39*
239	450	**3970**	09.02.40*	252	461	**3981**	31.07.39*

251	462	**3982**	28.02.40*	260	471	**3991**	28.02.40*
254	463	**3983**	29.04.39*	262	472	**3992**	13.09.39*
253	464	**3984**	31.07.39*	263	473	**3993**	18.07.39*
256	465	**3985**	17.11.38*	264	474	**3994**	27.10.39*
255	466	**3986**	03.01.39	265	475	**3995**	09.04.40*
257	467	**3987**	27.10.39*	266	476	**3996**	03.06.42
259	468	**3988**	03.05.49	267	477	**3997**	29.04.39*
258	469	**3989**	13.09.39*	268	478	**3998**	03.06.42
261	470	**3990**	29.04.39*	232	479	**3999**	31.01.39

Note * Converted to sleet locomotive – date shown is scrapping of saloon section of car.

CONTROL TRAILERS

"EALING" STOCK – Total 24

CLR No.	Built	Reno 1926–28	1930s No.	Disposal Date
62	1900 Ashbury	1882	5928	09.10.39
9	1900 Ashbury	1854	5934	27.10.39
18	1900 Ashbury	1857	5937	14.06.40
16	1900 Ashbury	1860	5940	18.10.39
17	1900 Ashbury	1862	5942	21.05.42
29	1900 Ashbury	1863	5943	10.11.39
33	1900 Ashbury	1865	5945	03.07.40
30	1900 Ashbury	1870	5950	31.07.39
58	1900 Ashbury	1871	5951	09.10.39
74	1900 Ashbury	1877	5957	25.06.40
51	1900 Ashbury	1878	5958	11.05.42
73	1900 Ashbury	1888	5964	19.01.39
94	1900 Ashbury	1889	5965	25.06.40
96	1900 Ashbury	1891	5967	21.10.42
103	1900 Ashbury	1893	5969	19.01.39
106	1900 Ashbury	1895	5971	18.10.39
90	1900 Ashbury	1898	5972	03.07.40
112	1900 Ashbury	1899	5973	03.07.40
105	1900 Ashbury	1904	5978	20.11.39
113	1900 Ashbury	1908	5982	11.05.42
154	1901 Ashbury	1909	5983	02.09.40
124	1900 Ashbury	1912	5986	29.04.39
150	1900 Brush	1914	5988	10.11.39
167	1901 Ashbury	1917	5991	31.01.39

"EALING" STOCK – YORKE CONVERSIONS
Converted in 1925 – Total 8

CLR No.	Built	Reno 1926–28	1930s No.	Disposal Date
6	1900 Ashbury	1852	5932	31.01.39
21	1900 Ashbury	1866	5946	25.06.40
37	1900 Ashbury	1867	5947	21.05.42
151	1901 Ashbury	1907	5981	10.11.39
119	1900 Ashbury	1910	5984	21.10.42
159	1901 Ashbury	1911	5985	04.09.39
160	1901 Ashbury	1913	5987	31.07.39
157	1901 Ashbury	1916	5990	03.07.40

"TUNNEL" STOCK – Total 40

CLR No.	Built		Reno 1926–28	1930s No.	Disposal Date
2	1900 Ashbury		1849	5929	09.10.39
4	1900 Ashbury	*	1850	5930	09.10.39
7	1900 Ashbury		1851	5931	09.10.39
13	1900 Ashbury	*	1853	5933	03.09.40
15	1900 Ashbury		1855	5935	02.09.40
11	1900 Ashbury	*	1856	5936	27.10.39
12	1900 Ashbury	*	1858	5938	12.06.40
19	1900 Ashbury	*	1859	5939	17.11.38
28	1900 Ashbury	*	1861	5941	12.06.40
20	1900 Ashbury		1864	5944	20.11.39
25	1900 Ashbury		1868	5948	17.06.42
56	1900 Ashbury	*	1869	5949	17.06.42
41	1900 Ashbury		1872	5952	18.10.39
63	1900 Ashbury		1873	5953	06.11.39
46	1900 Ashbury		1874	5954	20.11.39
64	1900 Ashbury	*	1875	5955	20.11.39
45	1900 Ashbury	*	1876	5956	06.11.39
83	1900 Ashbury	*	1879	5959	06.05.42
70	1900 Ashbury		1884	5960	17.06.42
85	1900 Ashbury	*	1883	5961	25.06.40
72	1900 Ashbury		1886	5962	02.09.40
89	1900 Ashbury	*	1887	5963	18.10.39
79	1900 Ashbury	*	1890	5966	14.06.40
82	1900 Ashbury	*	1894	5968	03.09.40
87	1900 Ashbury	*	1896	5970	06.05.42
92	1900 Ashbury	*	1900	5974	17.06.42
118	1900 Ashbury	*	1901	5975	03.07.40
98	1900 Ashbury	*	1902	5976	17.06.42

No.	Built		Reno	5000s No.	Disposal	No.	Built		Reno	5000s No.	Disposal
120	1900 Ashbury		1903	5977	14.06.40	169	1903 BRCW	*	1920	5994	14.06.40
147	1900 Brush		1905	5979	12.06.40	170	1903 BRCW	*	1919	5995	06.11.39
107	1900 Ashbury	*	1906	5980	06.11.39	54	1903 BRCW	*	1880	5996	14.06.40
161	1901 Ashbury	*	1915	5989	27.10.39	84	1903 BRCW	*	1881	5997	14.08.40
164	1901 Ashbury	*	1918	5992	12.06.40	81	1903 BRCW	*	1892	5998	02.09.40
109	1900 Ashbury		1897	5993	17.06.42	88	1903 BRCW	*	1885	5999	03.09.40

* First batch of control trailers converted 1908–09 and initially provided with front cab door roller shutters.

TRAILERS

"EALING" STOCK – Total 24

CLR No.	Built		Reno 1926–28	1930s No.	Disposal Date	CLR No.	Built		Reno 1926–28	1930s No.	Disposal Date
97	1900 Ashbury		1002	7902	19.01.39	148	1900 Brush		1039	7939	03.09.40
111	1900 Ashbury		1009	7909	19.01.39	149	1900 Brush		1040	7940	21.05.42
116	1900 Ashbury		1012	7912	10.11.39	162	1901 Ashbury		1046	7946	02.09.40
123	1900 Ashbury		1016	7916	31.01.39	163	1901 Ashbury		1047	7947	11.05.42
126	1900 Brush		1018	7918	27.10.39	31	1900 Ashbury		966	7966	09.10.39
128	1900 Brush		1020	7920	25.06.40	34	1900 Ashbury		968	7968	09.10.39
131	1900 Brush		1023	7923	31.01.39	42	1900 Ashbury		974	7974	20.11.39
133	1900 Brush		1025	7925	11.05.42	52	1900 Ashbury		980	7980	25.06.40
136	1900 Brush		1028	7928	03.06.42	59	1900 Ashbury		984	7984	20.11.39
138	1900 Brush		1030	7930	11.05.42	71	1900 Ashbury		992	7992	27.10.39
139	1900 Brush		1031	7931	10.01.39	80	1900 Ashbury		997	7997	06.11.39
143	1900 Brush		1035	7935	10.11.39	91	1900 Ashbury		999	7999	10.11.39

"TUNNEL" STOCK – Total 75

CLR No.	Built		Reno 1926–28	1930s No.	Disposal Date	CLR No.	Built		Reno 1926–28	1930s No.	Disposal Date
95	1900 Ashbury		1001	7901	29.11.38	153	1901 Ashbury		1042	7942	03.07.40
99	1900 Ashbury		1003	7903	06.05.42	155	1901 Ashbury		1043	7943	10.01.39
100	1900 Ashbury		1004	7904	02.09.40	156	1901 Ashbury		1044	7944	21.12.38
101	1900 Ashbury		1005	7905	21.05.42	158	1901 Ashbury		1045	7945	06.05.52
104	1900 Ashbury		1006	7906	21.05.42	165	1901 Ashbury		1048	7948	02.09.40
108	1900 Ashbury		1007	7907	17.11.38	166	1901 Ashbury		1049	7949	11.05.42
110	1900 Ashbury		1008	7908	06.05.42	168	1901 Ashbury		1050	7950	21.12.38
114	1900 Ashbury		1010	7910	21.10.42	84	1900 Ashbury	*	1051	7951	18.10.39
115	1900 Ashbury		1011	7911	18.10.39	88	1900 Ashbury	*	1052	7952	21.12.38
117	1900 Ashbury		1013	7913	12.06.40	43	1900 Ashbury		1053	7953	29.11.38
121	1900 Ashbury		1014	7914	08.12.38	93	1900 Ashbury		1000	7954	16.04.43
122	1900 Ashbury		1015	7915	27.10.39	1	1900 Ashbury		955	7955	21.12.38
125	1900 Ashbury		1017	7917	29.11.38	3	1900 Ashbury		956	7956	06.11.39
127	1900 Brush		1019	7919	08.12.38	5	1900 Ashbury		957	7957	03.01.39
129	1900 Brush		1021	7921	08.12.38	8	1900 Ashbury		958	7958	03.09.40
130	1900 Brush		1022	7922	03.07.40	10	1900 Ashbury		959	7959	03.01.39
132	1900 Brush		1024	7924	14.06.40	14	1900 Ashbury		960	7960	17.11.38
134	1900 Brush		1026	7926	29.11.38	22	1900 Ashbury		961	7961	08.12.38
135	1900 Brush		1027	7927	18.10.39	23	1900 Ashbury		962	7962	17.06.42
137	1900 Brush		1029	7929	20.11.39	24	1900 Ashbury		963	7963	04.09.39
140	1900 Brush		1032	7932	21.10.42	26	1900 Ashbury		964	7964	03.01.39
141	1900 Brush		1033	7933	03.09.40	27	1900 Ashbury		965	7965	03.01.39
142	1900 Brush		1034	7934	21.05.42	32	1900 Ashbury		967	7967	03.07.40
144	1900 Brush		1036	7936	03.09.40	35	1900 Ashbury		969	7969	14.07.39
145	1900 Brush		1037	7937	29.11.38	36	1900 Ashbury		970	7970	25.06.40
146	1900 Brush		1038	7938	06.05.42	38	1900 Ashbury		971	7971	10.01.39
152	1901 Ashbury		1041	7941	20.11.39	39	1900 Ashbury		972	7972	02.09.40

40† 1900 Ashbury	973	**7973**	04.09.39		65 1900 Ashbury	987	**7987**	03.08.40
44 1900 Ashbury	975	**7975**	06.11.39		66 1900 Ashbury	988	**7988**	12.06.40
47 1900 Ashbury	976	**7976**	25.06.40		67 1900 Ashbury	989	**7989**	10.11.39
48 1900 Ashbury	977	**7977**	06.11.39		68 1900 Ashbury	990	**7990**	12.06.40
49 1900 Ashbury	978	**7978**	17.06.42		69 1900 Ashbury	991	**7991**	27.10.39
50 1900 Ashbury	979	**7979**	08.12.38		75 1900 Ashbury	993	**7993**	28.08.39
53 1900 Ashbury	981	**7981**	18.10.39		76 1900 Ashbury	994	**7994**	10.01.39
55 1900 Ashbury	982	**7982**	03.08.39		77 1900 Ashbury	995	**7995**	27.10.39
57 1900 Ashbury	983	**7983**	12.06.40		78 1900 Ashbury	996	**7996**	08.12.38
60 1900 Ashbury	985	**7985**	29.04.39		86 1900 Ashbury	998	**7998**	29.11.38
61 1900 Ashbury	986	**7986**	14.06.40					

Notes

* Original cars 84 and 88 converted to motor cars (203 and 204) in 1902 and numbers taken by new BRCW trailers in 1903. They were converted back to trailers in 1906, becoming 171 and 172.

† Car 40 prototype air-door conversion in 1925.

LOCOMOTIVE CONVERSIONS

ELECTRIC SLEET LOCOMOTIVES – Total 18

Date Converted	No.	Former Nos	
22.12.38	ESL100	3960	3985
16.11.39	ESL101	3958	3983
21.10.39	ESL102	3990	3997
21.11.39	ESL103	3976	3979
11.11.39	ESL104	3971	3980
23.11.39	ESL105	3952	3965
29.11.39	ESL106	3984	3993
14.12.39	ESL107	3944	3981
23.12.39	ESL108	3989	3992
17.01.40	ESL109	3968	3972
14.02.40	ESL110	3987	3994
28.02.40	ESL111	3956	3959
29.03.40	ESL112	3945	3950
16.04.40	ESL113	3962	3969
11.05.40	ESL114	3967	3970
30.05.40	ESL115	3982	3991
21.06.40	ESL116	3953	3964
19.07.40	ESL117	3954	3995

DIESEL ELECTRIC LOCOMOTIVE

Date Converted	No.	Former Nos	
24.07.41	DEL120	3937	3941

CHAPTER TWO

1906 'GATE' TUBE STOCK

The original 'Gate' stock built in 1906–07 for the three tube lines (Bakerloo, Piccadilly and Hampstead – which were financed by the American entrepreneur Charles Tyson Yerkes) could all be described as basically 'similar' in appearance and operation. They were, however, built by several different car-builders and are summarised as follows:

		DM	T	CT	Total
Bakerloo	AC&F	36	36	36	108
Piccadilly	French	36	36	36	108
	Hungarian	36	36	36	108
Hampstead	AC&F	60	40	50	150
Piccadilly	Brush	–	1	–	1
(experimental)	MCCW	–	1	–	1
Total:		**168**	**150**	**158**	**476**

The cars were originally numbered as follows:

		DM	T	CT
Bakerloo	AC&F	1–36	201–236	101–136
Piccadilly	French	1–30, 61–66	201–230, 261–266	101–130, 161–166
	Hungarian	31–60, 67–72	231–260, 267–272	131–160, 167–172
Hampstead	AC&F	1–60	171–210	101–150
Piccadilly	Brush		291	
(experimental)	MCCW		292	

The pair of double-ended French motor cars stand coupled together at Holborn in 1947, whilst still at work on the Aldwych shuttle service. They were converted for this role in 1930, when the remainder of this type were withdrawn from service on the Piccadilly Line. *Author's collection*

The traffic offerings on the Piccadilly meant that the rolling stock provision was initially over-generous and many control trailer cars remained in stored condition for several years. Some were converted to motor cars for the Bakerloo Line, whilst others augmented train lengths. All were withdrawn by 1930.

For this book, we are concerned with those for the Piccadilly Line, but only those which were converted to air doors in the period 1920–1923 to run with new trailers and control trailers built in 1920 by Cammell Laird (q.v.). The need to enhance Piccadilly Line services after the First World War resulted in 20 Gate stock motor cars being converted to run with the new cars.

With air-door operation on tube cars then very much in its infancy, much was done on a trial and error basis. The converted motor cars still carried their original numbers and 20 cars were selected from the French-built batch, these being 2, 5–7, 10, 11, 14–18, 21, 23, 25–30 and 64.

The first two cars for conversion were sent to Cammell-Laird, who were building the new cars, in May 1920 and returned in November 1920, after which trials began. It was, however, another year or more before the first train entered service and even then extensive modifications had to be made to the original designs. The Gloucester RC&W Co. carried out the work on the other 18 cars, the first pair being despatched on 21 January 1922 (10 and 29), the last car (No. 27) on 7 July 1923 – the last to return on 3 October 1923. It was not until 20 December 1923 that the last of the converted motor cars and new cars had entered service. Even in converted form, the motor cars retained their original numbers until the LER renumbering scheme of 1926.

The first two motor cars (15 and 18) that were converted by Cammell-Laird in 1920 had a thick pillar between the doors, similar to the then new trailer counterparts. The first two Gloucester conversions (10 and 29) had single air-operated doors mounted on the outside of the car body, while the other 16 had single doors which slid back into (much neater) pockets, which was subsequently adopted as standard. To provide the motive power for the six experimental 'sample' trailers destined for the Hampstead Line, French air-door motor cars 21 and 26 were transferred from the Piccadilly to the Hampstead in the summer of 1923. Hitherto they were trialled on the Piccadilly Line, to where the motor cars returned in the autumn of 1924.

Even in converted form, the French motor cars retained their original numbers until the LER renumbering scheme of 1926. Early that year, they were renumbered in order from 480 to 499 but for some reason not entirely understood, the cars were numbered the 'wrong' way round. It had become the practice to indicate the direction in which the car faced by allocating odd or even numbers as appropriate. What became the Pre-1938 Tube Stock started the trend on the LER by allocating 'A' cars even numbers and 'B' cars odd numbers. By 1926 therefore, the system should have been well understood, but the converted cars all got the wrong numbers – it was perhaps an easy mistake, since almost all of the cars were renumbered in pairs as they were running at that time. One pair (492 and 499) even got the 'correct' number on 22 January 1926 but had to be renumbered three weeks later to conform with the others. This anomaly lasted until the cars were withdrawn from passenger service in 1929/30 and even later for those converted for other uses (q.v. below).

Whilst the Central London fleet was considered suitable for air-door conversion, the remainder of the 'Gate' stock was not, following some trials. The original plan proposed that all such cars were to be replaced with Pre-1938 Tube Stock, except for the 20 air-door motor cars running with the 1920 Cammell-Laird cars. However, in early 1929 a decision was taken to purchase 20 new motor cars to replace the French air-door motor cars to work with the 1920 trailers, which would then be suitably upgraded.

Interior of one of the French motor cars in June 1949. This had been converted to air-door operation in the early-1920s and to double-ended operation in 1930.
LT Museum

A total of 12 of the old converted air-door motor cars were scrapped in 1930, but six (480, 482, 483, 484, 485 and 497, ex–2, 6, 7, 10, 11 and 29 respectively) found further use as Ballast Motor cars on engineers train duties. These were converted in the summer of 1930, but even these cars were allocated 'wrong' numbers. The LPTB eventually corrected this in October 1936. In their dull grey livery as Ballast motors, the six comprised one car that had a centre door pillar (the Cammell-Laird conversion) and one car from the first Gloucester conversion (with its outside hung doors). Their replacement came in 1954/55 with the conversion of surplus Pre-1938 Tube Stock motor cars for similar work.

The remaining two motor cars (481 and 498, originally 5 and 30) were retained for passenger service on the Holborn–Aldwych shuttle, and were converted into double-ended cars. They were numbered (respectively) 186 and 185 in 1930, becoming 3282 and 3283 in 1933. Being maintained at Northfields depot (from 1932) they worked coupled together to and from the Aldwych branch and during the rush hour periods. In slack hours, however one car was sufficient and the other car was uncoupled and stabled in the overrun tunnel at Aldwych, acting as a 'spare' or 'rescue' car, should that in service develop a defect.

The Aldwych branch closed during the Second World War for economy reasons and the two motor cars were used on Tube Refreshment trains and also as pilot motor cars. They returned to passenger service when the branch line reopened after the war, but as time progressed, their appearance became spasmodic. By late-1949 they were withdrawn from passenger service but they often worked as pilot motor cars before being withdrawn for scrap in the mid-1950s.

DOUBLE-ENDED 'FRENCH' MOTOR CARS BUILT BY LES ATELIERS DE CONSTRUCTION DU NORD DE LA FRANCE, BLANC MISSERON, 1906

CONVERTED WITH AIR DOORS 1923 – Total 2

Original no.	Reno. 1926	Reno. 1930*	LPTB Reno.	Disposal
5	481	186	**3282**	17.12.56
30	498	185	**3283**	17.12.56

* Date converted to double-ended motors for Holborn–Aldwych shuttle.

CHAPTER THREE

1920 CAMMELL LAIRD TUBE STOCK

The 1920 Cammell Laird Tube Stock was novel in that it was the first production tube stock built with air-operated sliding doors. It was also unusual in that it continued to have the features of the last 'Gate' stock design – bulging sides, large windows and simple bogies with one brake block per wheel. It also had the first features of succeeding stocks – metal rimmed draughtscreens and air-worked doors. The original specification, however, was for hinged steel gates on the entrance platforms and swing side doors with electrically controlled locks. This was changed in September 1919 so that air doors were to be provided.

For the opening of the Piccadilly Line in 1906, a fleet of 36x6-car trains (216 cars) was provided for the line. Traffic did not develop as it was hoped and many of them lay idle for a number of years, with shorter train lengths operated than originally envisaged. As time progressed, the unused cars were used for other lines, mainly the Bakerloo, and by the end of the First World War, the Piccadilly Line was looking at additional stock to boost its own services – the 1920 Tube Stock was thus conceived. It was proposed that the Piccadilly Line should resume six-car train operation and 20 new trailers and control trailers were ordered in 1919 from Cammell Laird & Company of Nottingham. To operate with them, 20 French motor cars of 1906 vintage would be converted to air-door operation, to provide ten six-car trains.

A 1920 Cammell Laird control trailer stands at Queen's Park at the rear of a three-car Bakerloo Line train in 1935. These cars were among the last to be renumbered, 2047 becoming 5174 on 26 June 1935. The oval driving cab windows, fat post between the double doors and curve below waist level is evident. This stock was confined to working the Bakerloo Line 'local' service, not being suitable for outdoor working to Watford. These cars and the District 'F' stock had oval cab windows, a feature copied by the Berlin U-Bahn in 1923, but was not repeated thereafter. *Photomatic*

The 40 new cars were delivered to Lillie Bridge depot (the then depot for the Piccadilly Line), trailers first (numbered 800–819) in five batches of four cars from 19 November 1920 to 30 April 1921. The control trailers were delivered similarly, from 1 June 1921 to 17 August 1921. The fact that air-door operation was in its infancy resulted in a delay in converting the motor cars. The first pair, converted by Cammell Laird, were received back in December 1920, enabling trials to commence. These were extensive and it was another year before the first train carried passengers on the Piccadilly Line on 9 December 1921.

Nevertheless, progress was slow and none of the other 18 motor cars were sent for conversion until January 1922, the work being undertaken by the Gloucester Carriage and Wagon Company. Because the Piccadilly Line had 40 new cars, of which only four were in service, storage was a problem. The disused westbound track on the Aldwych branch served as a temporary home for ten trailers and ten control trailers from December 1921, which is where they remained until removed in June 1922 (eight cars) and September 1922 (12 cars). By this time, the converted motor cars were beginning to trickle back, although the last did not arrive until October 1923. The last of the Cammell Laird stock entered service on 20 December 1923, some three years since the first were delivered. The extensive delay was due in part to the fact in that the air-door equipment was extensively modified from the original design and only the four cars of the first train in service ever ran as originally designed.

The 1920 Cammell Laird cars had a pair of doors in the centre of the car, which were separated by a thick post, and single doors at the car ends. The driving cab ends had oval windows, which were also provided on the contemporary 'F' surface stock for the District Railway. The Underground authority in Berlin seems to have copied this feature, for the first generation of their large profile stock – the B1 class of 1923/24 – also had oval-shaped driving cab windows.

The cars when new were drab inside, being brown below the waist with a similar colour used for the upholstery – all seats were longitudinal. For standing passengers, horizontal grab rails were provided, suspended from the ceiling, rather than the traditional straps. Vertical grab rails were also provided in the seating area, but these were removed in early 1923, presumably being an inconvenience in the movement of passengers. The external livery was Derby red and the car numbers were shaded. An outside door cock was provided at the base of the thick pillar and a pilot lamp was provided at its top at the point where the curve of the roof began.

Because the new cars had to work with 1906 motor cars with BTH non-automatic electro-magnetic contactor control, the new Cammell Laird control trailers had to have similar matching control equipment. Therefore, from new, it is believed that this was acquired second-hand from 'Gate' stock former control trailers that had been converted to trailers.

Dissatisfaction with the interior features of the car led to one car being reconstructed in 1925, being provided with a bay of transverse seats in each half, new 'lozenge' moquette and improved lighting. However, only one car was so treated and it was another six years before the rest of the fleet followed suit. Meanwhile, the LER had devised a scheme to standardise car numbering and the Cammell Laird control trailers were renumbered in sequence in 1926 from 700–719 to 1700–1719, vacating number space needed for the new 1926 motor cars. Also in 1926, two six-car trains each comprising four Cammell Laird cars and two French air-door motor cars were loaned to the Central London Railway, to cover for its trains away for air-door conversion. The trains were transferred to their temporary home between June and September 1926, returning to the Piccadilly Line a year later. Difficulties arose on the CLR with the wheel profile and although the problems were resolved, the air-door trains appear to have been used only as a last resort, when no other CLR stock was available.

A further renumbering of the 40 Cammell Laird cars took place in 1930 because after various modifications they were more akin to the Pre-1938 Tube Stock rather than the older ex-Gate-Stock motors with which they had been working. The cars had also been painted in the then standard red/cream Underground livery. Trailers were renumbered from 800–819 to 1316–1335 and control trailers 1700–1719 to 2043–2062 – all in sequence.

The new Pre-1938 Tube Stock showed up the Cammell Laird stock to be drab and austere, the former having brightly lit green and yellow interiors with 'lozenge' pattern upholstery. In 1931 a decision was taken (replacing that abandoned in 1926) to modernise the Cammell Laird cars and convert them to work with newer motor cars which were ordered in 1929. The modernisation consisted of installing transverse seat bays in the centre of each section and adding armrests to the remaining longitudinal seats. Lighting was also upgraded and the cement flooring was replaced by grooved maple wood – even on the original car modernised in 1925, which had retained its original flooring.

Technical improvements included making the car compatible with the Pre-1938 stock motors, removing the guard's controls from control trailer cars, and making the driving cabs private. The double sliding doors on the cab ends were replaced by standard hinged communicating doors.

Following conversion, the cars were transferred from the Piccadilly Line to the Bakerloo, between January and October 1932, for use on the Queen's Park to Elephant and Castle 'local' service, although, following conversion they did work on the Piccadilly Line for a few months with newer motor cars. The reason for transfer away from the Piccadilly Line was that the line was to have much open-air running when its extensions opened, for which the stock was unsuitable. The Cammell Laird cars were also not designed for high speed running and whether the stock ever worked to Watford Junction is not known. The Bakerloo Line 'local' service, however, required 19x6-car trains and the Cammell Laird cars enabled about half of that service to be so provided and the remainder by complete trains of Pre-1938 Tube Stock.

Another new scheme resulted in the Cammell Laird cars being renumbered again, during 1934–35. This was devised before the formation of the LPTB in 1933 but it was adopted by them and involved all but a handful of passenger vehicles on the Underground. Trailers 1316–1319 became 7246–7249 and 1320–1335 became 7230–7245, while control trailers 2043–2062 became 5170–5189 in sequence, ironing out an anomaly in the numbering system created in 1930, where west facing cars were given odd numbers and east cars were given even. This was contrary to the normal practice, where 'A' (even numbered) cars faced west or north and 'B' (odd numbered and later 'D') cars faced east or south.

In the 1935–40 New Works Programme, only 16 Cammell Laird trailers were to continue in service, being earmarked for the Moorgate – Finsbury Park shuttle on the Northern City Line. Cars 7234–7249 were selected for this purpose and were fitted with electro-pneumatic brakes. Unlike other cars, they would not be fitted with 'passenger open' push buttons, along with their nominated motor cars. The plans failed to come to fruition, initially because they were found to be out of gauge on the Northern City Line. This resulted in an unplanned but hasty reshuffle of stock requirements and spelt the end for the Cammell Laird stock. The first cars, however, had been withdrawn from Bakerloo service as early as September 1938.

The Second World War was the other major factor in the future of the Cammell Laird stock. But for this, it would probably have gone for scrap, but along with many other tube cars awaiting line extensions that had been deferred because of hostilities, all 40 were put into store, some assuming less glamorous roles than intended. Five control trailers were utilised as ARP shelters (5170, 5184, and 5187 at Cockfosters, with 5182 and 5189 at Ealing Common) while four cars were moved to the Northern Line and put into store in open sidings at Edgware in 1944. Quite why the latter occurred remains a mystery. Some cars are believed to have been painted grey during the war years.

Once hostilities had ceased, it was decided to scrap all but five of the Cammell Laird cars, the majority thus not being suitable for post-war Underground use. To that end they were disposed of between July 1946 and November 1948, being taken to the Steel Breaking and Dismantling Company's scrap yard near Chesterfield.

The five cars that were retained were converted into a mobile instruction train for rolling stock staff. It was intended that the motive power would be provided by a pair of 1903 Central London motor cars specially converted but this was not pursued and the two cars set aside were scrapped (q.v. Chapter 2). Because Acton Works was fully committed to routine overhaul and repair work, and the rehabilitation of Pre-1938 Tube Stock for the Central Line, the conversion work was undertaken at Hammersmith depot on the Metropolitan Line. In their new livery of dull orange, work was completed in November 1949. The interiors were gutted and refitted with relevant equipment for instruction purposes – blackboard and epidiascope in a 'classroom', three sets of traction control, e.p. braking system, an automatic wedgelock coupler and a pair of air-operated doors complete with guard's control panel. Other teaching aids included cut away items of equipment placed on benches, plus train equipment diagrams. An air compressor was provided for the pneumatically-operated mechanisms and a motor generator for the electrical equipment and the three cars that were fitted with fluorescent lighting.

The majority of the Cammell Laird cars therefore had a short history – they were scrapped being less than 30 years old and had performed only about 18 years of revenue earning service. The Instruction train, however, kept their memory alive in the post-war London Transport, and at least two cars 'scrapped' were sold onwards to a company in Brownhills in Staffordshire, used possibly as laboratories at one time.

1920 CAMMELL LAIRD STOCK – BUILT 1920

CONTROL TRAILERS – Total 20

Original No.	Reno. 1926	Reno. 1930	Reno. 1934–35	Wartime location/status	Conversion	Disposal date
700	1700	2043	**5170**	ARP Cockfosters	IC1075 15.11.49	
701	1701	2044	**5171**	Cockfosters		18.11.46
702	1702	2045	**5172**	Cockfosters		08.01.48
703	1703	2046	**5173**	Cockfosters		08.01.48
704	1704	2047	**5174**	Cockfosters*		10.11.48
705	1705	2048	**5175**	Cockfosters		30.07.46
706	1706	2049	**5176**	Cockfosters		08.01.48
707	1707	2050	**5177**	Cockfosters		08.01.48
708	1708	2051	**5178**	Cockfosters		18.11.46
709	1709	2052	**5179**	Cockfosters		30.07.46
710	1710	2053	**5180**	Cockfosters		18.11.46
711	1711	2054	**5181**	Cockfosters		18.11.46
712	1712	2055	**5182**	ARP Ealing Common		30.07.46
713	1713	2056	**5183**	Cockfosters		18.11.46
714	1714	2057	**5184**	ARP Cockfosters		20.04.48
715	1715	2058	**5185**	Cockfosters*		10.11.48
716	1716	2059	**5186**	Cockfosters		08.01.48
717	1717	2060	**5187**	ARP Cockfosters		20.04.48
718	1718	2061	**5188**	Cockfosters		18.11.46
719	1719	2062	**5189**	ARP Ealing Common		30.07.46

TRAILERS – Total 20

Original No.	Reno. 1930	Reno. 1934–35	Wartime location/status	Conversion	Disposal date
804	1320	**7230**	Cockfosters		30.07.46
805	1321	**7231**	Cockfosters*		10.11.48
806	1322	**7232**	Ealing Common		30.07.46
807	1323	**7233**	Cockfosters*		10.11.48
808	1324	**7234**	Cockfosters		27.07.47
809	1325	**7235**	Cockfosters	IC1079 15.11.49	
810	1326	**7236**	Cockfosters		27.07.47
811	1327	**7237**	Ealing Common		10.11.48
812	1328	**7238**	Cockfosters		20.04.48
813	1329	**7239**	Cockfosters		20.04.48
814	1330	**7240**	Cockfosters		27.07.47
815	1331	**7241**	Cockfosters	IC1078 15.11.49	
816	1332	**7242**	Cockfosters		20.04.48
817	1333	**7243**	Cockfosters	IC1076 15.11.49	
818	1334	**7244**	Ealing Common		10.11.48
819	1335	**7245**	Cockfosters		27.07.47
800	1316	**7246**	Cockfosters		27.07.47
801	1317	**7247**	Cockfosters		20.04.48
802	1318	**7248**	Cockfosters	IC1077 15.11.49	
803	1319	**7249**	Cockfosters		27.07.47

* To store at Edgware by 22.06.44

Opposite Interior of a Cammell Laird trailer car in May 1939. The interiors had changed considerably since new, having been refurbished in the early-1930s. This included fitting transverse seats, leather armrests on longitudinal seats, swan-neck light fittings at cantrail level and maple wood flooring. *LT Museum*

CHAPTER FOUR

Pre-1938 'STANDARD' TUBE STOCK

By 1920 it had been decided to extend the City and South London Railway at both ends and similarly the Hampstead Tube Line. Because of the layout of the two lines, it was natural for them to be joined and worked as one railway. As the City & South London was the first proper 'tube' railway, its tunnels were smaller than those of the Hampstead (and other tube lines), and they had to be enlarged and reconstructed before joining with the Hampstead. The C&SLR's unique locomotives and carriages would have to be replaced and the Hampstead's 'Gate' stock also came under scrutiny – modernise or be replaced. This gave possible opportunities for large orders of new trains and to that end, a wooden mock up was constructed at Golders Green depot incorporating as many different features as possible. This included cab window design, one being oval as on the 1920 Cammell Laird tube stock and District Line 'F' stock, the other being rectangular with an upward curved top – it was the latter that was subsequently adopted.

In August 1922 the Underground Electric Railways of London ordered five trailers and one control trailer from five separate companies to enable a final design to be chosen for the bulk of the new stock orders. The builders were given a free hand in design and finish, save for the basic criteria to be adhered to in tube car construction, apart from the control trailer, whose specifications were laid down by the Underground's engineering staff. In an attempt to reduce train noise in tunnels, a number of experiments were also made with sound baffles around the area of the bogies.

The Cammell Laird motors and control trailers of Pre-1938 Tube Stock were all of a similar design, having more rounded tops to the driving cab windows than those built by other companies. The 1925 Cammell Laird cars differed, however, in having triangular ventilation scoops above the saloon windows rather than rectangular as on the 1923 cars. DM 3619 is seen in Wood Lane depot, one of several cars set aside for 'Tube Refreshment' duties during the Second World War. *Charles F. Klapper/LURS*

The Gloucester R&CW Co. built the control trailer and one trailer, the other (trailers) were built by Leeds Forge, Metropolitan Carriage Wagon & Finance Co., Birmingham RC & W Co., and Cammell Laird and Co. Each of the six prototype cars had a continuous clerestory from one end to the other. In summary, the six cars were described variously as 'tube cars deluxe' and 'Underground Pullman specials', each one being different in some form or another. Perhaps the most exotic car was the Gloucester trailer which had ornate light fittings along the centre of the ceiling with bell shaped lamp shades. Another ornate offering was the trailer from Birmingham which had slightly less ornate light fittings but nevertheless upmarket. The central ceiling panels of this car were white with decorated edging. The other cars were less decorative, although they were individualistic. The ceiling of the Gloucester control trailer, for example had embossed ornamentation on a linen-textured ground. The Leeds Forge trailer had 18 ceiling-mounted lights in glass bowls, with two more being provided to illuminate a ceiling car line diagram midway down the car. In contrast, the Cammell Laird car had 70 lamps, many being concealed in troughs along the monitor rail and covered with translucent panels, which enabled good illumination of the adverts. There were individual lamps in the doorway area. The interior of the Gloucester control trailer and the MCCW trailer were more recognisable as tube cars, but the latter had lamps recessed into the bodywork and both still had some ornate features.

The six cars were delivered to Lillie Bridge depot in January 1923 and began trials on the Piccadilly Line using French air door motor cars as motive power. All cars, plus two French motor cars, were transferred to the Hampstead Line in the summer of 1923, where they operated until the production series began, which enabled the motor cars to be returned to the Piccadilly Line.

The trials of these prototype cars resulted in orders for new cars, which turned out to be the biggest group of stock to operate on the Underground. At maximum the fleet comprised 1,466 cars built over a 12 year period between 1922 and 1934, involving many separate orders and, sample cars excepted, involved five different car builders. In simplistic terms for identification purposes, they can be divided into three groups – 1923–25, 1926–30 and 1931–34. There were, however, numerous detail differences between them and although becoming known collectively as the Pre-1938 Tube stock or 'Standard' tube stock, it was many years before the latter title could be genuinely applied. The different orders are best summarised in the table below. In all, there were 645 driving motor cars, 551 trailers and 270 control trailers.

End year	As delivered					In service				
	M	CT	T	Year total	Stock total	M	CT	T	Year total	Stock total
1923	3	1	23	27	27	–	1	9	10	10
1924	78	35	57	170	197	79	35	71	185	195
1925	47	22	21	90	287	15	10	5	30	225
1926	53	70	34	157	444	67	77	50	194	419
1927	–	–	18	18	462	20	5	–	25	444
1928	120	11	118	249	711	80	6	127	213	657
1929	131	93	109	333	1044	147	98	118	363	1020
1930	20	18	21	59	1103	43	12	20	75	1095
1931	42	20	20	82	1185	23	26	21	70	1165
1932	125	–	130	255	1440	106	–	96	202	1367
1933	–	–	–	–	1440	39	–	34	73	1440
1934	18	–	–	18	1458	9	–	–	9	1449
1935	8	–	–	8	1466	17	–	–	17	1466
Total:	645	270	551	1466	1466	645	270	551	1466	1466

Cars were owned by the LER, except for those listed below, which were owned by the C&SLR. The creation of the LTPB in 1933 thus made one owner for them all.

1923	MCCW Motors	553–580	28
	MCCW CTs	743–755	13
	Birmingham Trailers	872–899	28
1924	MCCW Motors	581–593	13
	CL CTs	1756–1761	6
	Birmingham Trailers	900–911	12
1925 (1)	CL Motors	643–647	5
	MCCW CTs	1800–1808	9
			114

A feature of the six 'sample' cars was the continuous clerestory. On all production trains, the clerestory was stopped over the passenger door areas, enabling a more gentle curve of the doors with the roof line and increasing headroom. On the 1923 cars the clerestory was continuous over the guard's door (motor cars) and side cab door (control trailers), a feature that was discontinued on subsequent builds of stock. Headlights were arranged in pairs on either side of the front cab door but towards the outer edges. The lights were illuminated all the time the train was in service but when not required for display were covered by hinged shutters.

The Cammell Laird cars had curved edges to the clerestory, which enabled the rectangular ventilators to be fully seen. On the MCCW and the Birmingham cars, the clerestory had eaves under which were fitted sloping ventilator scoops. The MCCW cars had semi-elliptical rain strips over the doors, the Cammell Laird cars had straight rain strips and the Birmingham cars also straight but pointing downwards at the ends.

The 1923 Cammell Laird cars were the mainstay of the Northern Line until replaced by 1938 Tube Stock, and then, from the late-1930s, on the Central and Northern City lines. A few made an appearance on the Piccadilly Line, as illustrated by 7288 at Rayners Lane, which came onto the line in October 1942 and stayed there until scrapped in 1954. It should be noted that by this time, much less use was made of the cream colour, it being confined to around the windows and no longer extending to the ends of the cars. *Author's collection*

All 1923–25 motors and control trailer cars were provided with destination blinds above the front cab door. Ventilation took the form of small sections just above floor level on the trailing ends of the 1923 cars along with pull-down main car windows. On the 1924 cars tilting quarter lights were provided instead with ventilation slots on the trailing ends, immediately below cantrail height.

Ventilation louvres were provided in pairs on each side of the equipment compartments on the Cammell Laird DMs, a smaller pair in line with them were provided on the curved roof area. The MCCW motor cars were similar but the main louvre pairs were closer together and on the roof curve there were four smaller louvres rather than two wide ones. All trains had a crew of driver and three guards.

On all 1924 cars rain strips were additionally provided over the passenger windows and between cars, chains had given way to grab rails – now a similar system (known as Inter Car Barriers) has been fitted to new stock and existing ones, this 'circle' having been fully 'turned' after 75 years! The 1924 cars incorporated the outside door cock at floor level in a circular recess. The BRCW trailers were first delivered with the slanting ventilator scoops under the eaves which faced in alternate directions. During the build this was changed so that they were in groups of three equally spaced, all facing one way on one side, and the opposite way on the other. The MCCW and BRCW cars had ribbing introduced on passenger doors which resulted in the door guide wheels at floor level standing proud – the doors were a single aluminium casting. The 1924 Cammell Laird cars, however, continued with 'flush' doors but instead of having rectangular roof line vents, were provided with triangular ventilation scoops that were not covered by the clerestory. These cars also had rain strips over passenger windows but not over the side cab doors. At the trailing ends of the car narrow horizontal ventilation slots were provided on each side of and over the communicating doors.

Cammell Laird built all the motor cars of the two 1925 batches, with MCCW providing all the trailers and control trailers. The motor cars were similar to their 1923 counterparts but had the triangular ventilation scoops over the passenger windows, tilting quarter lights and rain strips over the passenger windows as with the 1924 cars, but introduced door ribbing on the new cars. The MCCW trailers and control trailer cars continued with clerestory eaves right to the car ends, except for the driving end of control trailers, where an arch roof was provided – on all cars since 1924 the clerestory stopped where there were side (passenger, cab or guard's) doors – sliding or hinged. This batch of stock was the last to be built with destination blinds, thick waistbands, slightly recessed windows and pairs of headlights separated by a centre cab door. The 1925 control trailers were the last to be equipped with guard's door controls and these were later removed.

The cars introduced from 1926 saw many changes to what had gone before. The offside cab window was shallower than that provided for the driver, two-line destination plates were provided underneath and a group of four headlights underneath them. Interior shutters were provided to enable the relevant code to be displayed. The clerestory eave was retained only over the equipment compartment at the driving cab end, the other sections of the clerestory on all cars being provided without, exposing the triangular ventilation scoops. On the contactor side of the equipment compartment, plain metal sheeting replaced the grilles, giving a rather uneven appearance. This batch of stock was the first not to have the cream livery applied around the car ends – all saloon car windows were flush with the body sides and there were no rain strips provided above them. Train telephone communication between the driver and guard had been developed so it was incorporated on this stock – the others were subsequently retrofitted. This enabled the train crew to be reduced to two – a driver and a (rear) guard. The interior layouts were unchanged, but these and the following cars lacked the ornate and sometimes 'fussy' features of their predecessors.

The Pre-1938 stock was ideal for use as pilot motor cars, as it was operated on an individual 'car' basis rather than on a semi-permanent 'unit' basis as with later stocks. During the Second World War, when these cars were plentiful because of the non-completion of the 1935–40 New Works Programme, some were painted in service stock grey livery. 1924 MCCW DM 3564 was thus treated and is seen in Morden depot on 16th May 1948 with a similarly-painted partner. *Alan B. Cross*

Like the previous batch, the two 1927 builds were by MCCW. Those for the Hampstead Line with GEC equipment were almost identical to their immediate predecessors, but the Piccadilly Line batch with BTH equipment lacked ribbing on the passenger doors. Cab fronts on both motor and control trailers were still devoid of any ventilators.

The next build of stock was dependent on the Bakerloo Line's gate stock being withdrawn rather than being converted to air door operation. The former decision was the one taken with new trains being the more economical option. This batch of stock closely followed the 1927 design but there were differences. Built by the Union Construction and Finance Company, the most distinguishing feature was probably the slight bodyside 'bulge' below waist level. Rain strips over passenger (only) doors were straight and there were even minor internal detail differences, the most noticeable being the door separating the saloon from the equipment compartment, which was more plainly finished. One of the 1928 UCC cars was finished differently from the others, pending possible changes to forthcoming stock orders; the most obvious was the lack of a centre door pillar. The clerestory was rounded and ventilation was provided under the rounded eaves without scoops – no variation was made over the equipment compartment, taking it right to the cab end. Inside, additional grilles were fitted to the outer edges of the ceiling, while the tilting quarter lights were protected at the top by narrow glass strips. Standard vents were retained on the clerestory risers.

Resulting from this experiment, it was decided that a subsequent batch of 20 UCC motor cars should not be fitted with the centre door pillars – always considered a hindrance in the flow of passengers. In all other respects they were identical to the first batch, none of the other features then being adopted. These 20 cars were designated as replacements for the same number of French air-door motor cars.

A third batch of stock from UCC at Feltham followed in 1929. These were the first to be fitted with electro-pneumatic brakes and until other earlier cars were similarly equipped, they were kept in block train sets on the Piccadilly Line. Like the previous batch of 20 motor cars there was no centre door pillar but the doors were flush panelled. The only other design change was to the vents over the equipment compartment on the roof curve – louvres had given way to rectangular covers which were open at the base, curved in line with the roof with their top ends fitting snugly under the clerestory eave.

The last tube rolling stock to be built at Feltham by UCC in fact comprised one six car train. It was a prototype prior to the final decisions being taken for the extra trains needed for the Piccadilly Line extensions. It was truly 'Feltham' in having the traditional curved panels below waist level and straight rain strips, but each of the cars had new features. Because of the country's financial crisis of the time and the campaign to 'buy British', it was known as the 'All British Train'. The train consisted of four trailers and two motors, the latter having air operated guard's doors rather than hinged and hand-operated. These single doors slid back into glazed pockets and this window thus had no opening quarter lights.

Two of the trailers followed previous layouts in having two pairs of doors, but were wider to improve boarding and alighting times. These doors were moved inwards to the car centre slightly and as a result, the centre bay had only three windows instead of four. The other two trailers of the prototype train had standard pairs of doors with four windows between them, but with wide single doors at the ends, sliding back into glazed pockets. In the end bays, there was one non-opening casement window and one window with opening quarter lights. There were no ventilation scoops but vents into the cars were provided under rounded eaves.

From May 1939, Pre-1938 Tube Stock began operating on the Northern City Line, replacing the original trains of 1904–06 that were built to 'main line' size. Apart from the open station at Drayton Park, this short branch line was in tunnel throughout. 1927 MCCW motor car 3406 is seen in Drayton Park depot soon after the conversion. Note that the 1923 Cammell Laird trailer (second vehicle) has the cream painted section right to the end of the car. *Charles F. Klapper/LURS*

Whilst the extra doors improved passenger flows, seating was reduced by eight to 40. Because all six cars were marginally longer than their predecessors, the car ends tapered inwards to negotiate curves in the tunnels. All cars had for the first time proper ventilators over the communicating and front cab doors, and interior car heaters.

The trains operating the Bakerloo service to Watford Junction were new in 1920 and were owned jointly by LER/LNWR (LER/LMS from 1923). However, they had swing doors with electric locks and did not match the superior performance of the Pre-1938 Tube Stock, which replaced the Gate Stock in 1929. Therefore, it was decided to replace the 1920 cars with new stock and MCCW supplied ten six-car trains plus two spare motors (because the rolling stock could be uncoupled individually, it was always the practice to order more motors than trailers, enabling easy swapping of cars in the event of defects). In most respects they were copies of the 1927 MCCW stock, but from new they lacked door pillars on motor cars, all passenger doors were flush, and ventilators were provided over the communicating and front cab doors. Unlike the 1929 UCC motor cars, grilles returned to the roof over the equipment compartment. This batch of stock effectively completed the second generation of what became the Pre-1938 Tube Stock.

The cars built from 1926 represented the second generation of Pre-1938 Tube Stock, having more flush panelling, and headlights and destination boxes located under the offside front cab window. Seen at Epping in the early-1950s is a pair of 1926 MCCW DMs operating a shuttle service between there and Loughton. When the Central Line first reached Epping in 1949, the service was provided by alternate 'through' and 'shuttle' trains. *John H. Meredith*

A 1927 MCCW DM leads a four-car train into Acton Town, after uncoupling was reintroduced on the Piccadilly Line on 12 May 1952. It will be noted that passenger-open push buttons were fitted to this car, but the operation of passenger door control was never used on the Piccadilly Line. *F.G. Reynolds*

The third generation of stock comprised just two batches, the first in 1931 provided for the Piccadilly's eastern and western extensions. The best features were taken from the 1930 UCC experimental train and the order was shared between MCCW (145 motors), BRCW and GRCW (90 and 40 trailers respectively). The motor cars had air-operated guard's doors and the end window section at the trailing end provided the pockets for them to slide into. Therefore, the clerestory stopped short and only two ventilation scoops were fitted into this end of the car. Both ends tapered inwards, as these were slightly longer than the older cars and at the corners the cantrail beading lines met at an angle, rather than providing the graceful curve of the earlier cars built by MCCW, BRCW and GRWC. Being designed for open air running, window wipers were fitted. Below the waist line, the body sides were flat. Because the guard's doors were air-operated, the control panels were located on the end wall with a centre pilot light underneath the ventilation grille and above the communicating doors. On the previous stocks the guard's panel was on the wall dividing his area from the saloon, necessitating the guard to operate the buttons behind him when looking to the front of the train.

The two batches of 1931 trailers were indistinguishable. They were based on the 1930 experimental trailers with end doors but a more even finish was created by having end single doors half the width of the doubles, reorganising the centre section of the cars to have four windows instead of three and similarly at each end, which had three windows instead of two. No ventilation scoops were provided but a rounded edge clerestory for ventilation was provided over the windows with tilting quarter lights. To partly compensate for the loss of eight seats on six-doors-aside trailers, four pull-down tip up seats were provided at the ends, one on each side of the communicating door. Because many of these cars were delivered in advance of the completed extension, some worked on the District shuttles (Acton Town to Hounslow and South Harrow) from February 1932.

The final order for Pre-1938 Tube Stock was for 26 motor cars in 1934. They joined their 1931 counterparts, on the Piccadilly Line, which enabled some older cars to be transferred to the Hampstead Line to provide more seven-car trains. The 1934 motor cars were almost identical to the 1931 batch and the only noticeable differences on them was that the quarter lights were gravity-operated rather than spring toggle, and minor changes were made to equipment layout in the cab.

Date	Builder	Car type		Original numbering	1930s numbering	Car totals			Notes
1922	Gloucester	CT		720	5271	1			'Competition' or
	Gloucester	T		820	7270	1			'Sample' stock
	Leeds Forge	T		821	7271	1			
	Met. Carriage	T		822	7272	1			
	Birmingham	T		823	7273	1			
	Cammell Laird	T		824	7274	1	6	6	
1923	Cammell Laird	M	(MV)	500–538	3446–3484	39			C&SLR replacement
	Cammell Laird	M	(GEC)	539–540	3445–3444	2			and Edgware extension
	Cammell Laird	T	(MV)	825–864	7275–7314	40			stock The 'Competition'
	Met. Carriage	M	(MV)	541–580	3485–3524	40			stock was also
	Met. Carriage	CT	(MV)	721–755	5211–5245	35			considered part of this
	Birmingham	T	(MV)	865–899	7315–7349	35	191	197	batch
1924	Met. Carriage	M	(MV)	581–587	3525–3531	7			Kennington & Morden
	Met. Carriage	M	(GEC)	588–632	3532–3576	45			extension stock
	Birmingham	T	(GEC)	900–949	7350–7399	50			
	Cammell Laird	CT	(MV)	1756–1769	5246–5259	14			
	Cammell Laird	CT	(GEC)	1770–1780	5260–5270	11	127	324	
1925 (I)	Cammell Laird	M	(GEC)	633–647	3577–3587				Kennington & Morden
					3621–3624	15			additional stock
	Met. Carriage	CT	(GEC)	1782–1808	5272–5298	27	42	366	
1925 (II)	Cammell Laird	M	(GEC)	648–680	3588–3620	33			Hampstead additional
	Met. Carriage	CT	(GEC)	1809–1848	5299–5338	40			stock and stock for
	Met. Carriage	T	(GEC)	950–954	7400–7404	5	78	444	covering air-door conversion of CLR stock
1926	Met. Carriage	M	(GEC)	681–744	3625–3688	64			Hampstead additional
	Met. Carriage	T	(GEC)	1054–1101	7405–7452	48	112	556	stock
1927 (I)	Met. Carriage	M	(GEC)	329–391	3381–3441	63			Hampstead 'Gate' stock
	Met. Carriage	T	(GEC)	1102–1208	7453–7558				replacement
					7570	107	170	726	

Date	Builder	Car type		Original numbering	1930s numbering	Car totals			Notes
1927 (II)	Met. Carriage	M	(BTH)	282–328	3312–3341				Piccadilly 'Gate' stock replacement
					3364–3380	47			
	Met. Carriage	CT	(BTH)	1921–1956	5137–5152				
					5339–5359	36			
	Met. Carriage	T	(BTH)	1209–1261	7000–7016				
					7190–7214				
					7559–7569	53	136	862	
1928	UCC Feltham	M	(BTH)	225–281	3038–3067				Bakerloo 'Gate' stock replacement
					3284–3311	57			
		CT	(BTH)	1957–2024	5000–5100				
					5153–5169	68			
		T	(BTH)	1262–1298	7017–7038				
					7215–7229	37	162	1024	
1928	UCC Feltham	M	(BTH)	205–224	3018–3037	20	20	1044	French air-door motor car replacement
1929	UCC Feltham	M	(BTH)	187–204	3000–3017	18			Hampstead additional stock actually replaced 1927 stock transferred Piccadilly to Hampstead
	UCC Feltham	CT	(BTH)	2025–2042	5102–5136	18			
	UCC Feltham	T	(BTH)	1299–1315	7039–7055	17	53	1097	
1930	UCC Feltham	M	(BTH)	183–184	3069–3068	2			Piccadilly experimental stock
	UCC Feltham	T	(BTH)	1336–1339	7056–7059	4	6	1103	
1930	Met. Carriage	M	(BTH)	161–182	3342–3363	22			Watford (Bakerloo) replacement stock
	Met. Carriage	CT	(BTH)	2063–2082	5190–5209	20			
	Met. Carriage	T	(BTH)	1340–1359	7250–7269	20	62	1165	
1931	Met. Cammell	M	(BTH)	–	3070–3281	145			Piccadilly extension stock
	Birmingham	T	(BTH)	–	7060–7149	90			
	Gloucester	T	(BTH)	–	7150–7189	40	275	1440	
1934	Met. Cammell	M	(BTH)	–	3689–3721	26	26	1466	Piccadilly additional stock

The gaps in 1930s numbering were filled by older cars, viz. 3282–3283 (1906 'Aldwych' cars), 5170–5189 (1920 Cammell Laird CTs) and 7230–7249 (1920 Cammell Laird trailers).

The earliest types of stock (1923–27) on the Hampstead line were all compatible, but when electro pneumatic brakes were introduced, these were unable to work with Westinghouse only braked cars. A considerable number of stock transfers between lines took place in the 1929–31 period as a result of conversions and modifications, the end result being that the Pre-1938 Tube Stock would become 'Standard' stock, which it would later be named.

The last 20 motor cars built in 1928 by the UCC at Feltham were the first motor cars of this type not to have centre door pillars. One such car leads a seven-car train on the Piccadilly Line at Rayners Lane. *LT Museum*

The refinements made to the 1929 batch of Pre-1938 Tube Stock are apparent on this motor car of a four-car train at Sudbury Town. This was built in 1929 by UCC at Feltham. Gently curving ventilator scoops have replaced grilles over the equipment compartment and centre door pillars have been abolished. *F.G. Reynolds*

Changes, improvements and experiments to the cars in the 1930s included:

- The fitting of e.p. brakes to most cars by mid-1935, the only motor cars still with Westinghouse brakes being those allocated to the Bakerloo Line 'local' service working with 1920 Cammell Laird trailers.

- Destination plates and four headlights fitted to the 1923–25 cars under the offside cab window, with destination blinds and headlight pairs removed. On CT cars, however, the original headlights were retained.

- Ventilators were fitted above communicating doors and above cab doors on the 1923–29 stocks.

- Grab rails replaced chains at car ends on 1923-built cars, although some survived with them. Other stocks had grab rails from new.

- Trials with line names at various positions on car sides – not continued with. A wide blue stripe was provided between waist and cant rail height on Bakerloo Line trains that worked to Watford Junction between 1934 and 1937.

- Train set numbers relocated at the bottom of the offside front cab window. When the 'weak field' yellow and black striped flag was added later, the number plates were moved up higher on brackets.

- A 'streamlined' cab front fitted to 1923 MCCW control trailer 1755 in early 1933 prior to the construction of the 1935 'streamlined' stock.

- With the future streamlined stock in mind, experimental automatic couplers by Tomlinson were fitted to CTs 5012 and 5046 in 1933. They were not suited to the rigours of Underground working and future trials took place in 1934 on 1927 MCCW control trailers 1944 (old number) and 5151 with G.D. Peters equipment.

- Air-conditioning trials on 1927 MCCW trailer 7195 in 1935.

- Nine car train operation on the Northern Line from 8 November 1937 – the Hampstead (& City) Line had since become the Morden-Edgware Line and the Northern Line from 28 August 1937. These trains were formed M-T-M+T-T-T+M-T-M and at tube tunnel stations either the leading two or rear two cars were required to stop in the tunnel according to the relevant instructions. The guard travelled on the seventh car and was able to isolate doors as appropriate. These trains were restricted to operating between Kennington and Colindale via Charing Cross, extended to Edgware from 7 February 1938. The first nine-car train was formed 3390–7486–3679+7452–7545–7430+3400–7517–3339.

- All the Pre-1938 Tube Stock was renumbered according to a plan drawn up by the LER in 1930. This was often erroneously referred to as 'LPTB numbering' as renumbering began in 1931 and took four years to achieve. The new 1931–34 cars were numbered in the new series and the chance was taken to ensure all 'A' cars had even numbers and 'B' cars ('D' cars from mid-1937) had odd numbers. Motor cars were renumbered 3xxx, control trailers 5xxx and trailers 7xxx. The Piccadilly Line extensions resulted in many transfers of cars between lines and to meet the relevant stock requirements 34 'B' end CTs were converted to 'A' end between 1931 and 1933.

- Short train operation of three cars with only one motor car was abandoned on the Piccadilly Line in 1936, because it was not desirable to have a train with just one compressor. If this failed in service a lengthy delay would ensue while the defective set was removed from service. All short trains were henceforth formed M-T-T-M. Other lines subsequently followed suit apart from the Northern City Line which continued with the practice – this was a short branch line which would inconvenience few if such a problem occurred. After the outbreak of the Second World War, the operation of short trains in slack hours was discontinued on all lines except the Northern City, to save on staffing costs.

The £40 million 1935–40 New Works Programme resulted in new 1938 Tube Stock for the Northern Line, enabling the transfer of the Pre-1938 Tube Stock from that line to the Central, which was to be extended at its eastern and western ends. Pre-1938 stock was also transferred to the Northern City Line replacing its original 1904–06 stock built to 'main line' size, as well as increasing train lengths on the Bakerloo. A number of conversions and general updating of the Pre-1938 Tube Stock features were undertaken and are summarised thus:

- All trains destined for the Central Line would be fitted with car heaters, passenger door control and braking improvements. They would all pass through Acton Works before taking up service on the Central Line, having been overhauled and modified.

- 90 control trailers to be converted to trailers, removing redundant equipment from the cabs. The 5xxx numbers would be prefixed by a '7' on conversion.

- The 20 motor cars which had been running with Cammell Laird trailers would be equipped with e.p. brakes and become standard with the rest of the Pre-1938 stock.

- 58 trailers of 1927 stock to be converted to run with the new 1938 Tube Stock. These would be fitted with compressors and 50V lighting circuits. Once converted they worked on both the Northern and Bakerloo Lines, although by 1941 they were all on the latter.

- Because of the stock imbalance of operating seven-car trains with the four-car set at the 'A' end, 26 DMs were to be turned and converted from 'A' to 'D' end cars.

Piccadilly Line services were extended to Uxbridge in October 1933, replacing District Line shuttle services and through services to London were thus provided by Piccadilly and Metropolitan Line trains by different routes. Arriving at the old Uxbridge terminus in Belmont Road is DM 3144, built in 1931 by Metropolitan Cammell – a new station was opened in Uxbridge High Street in 1938. In the background can be seen Park Road bridge, still a notable landmark in Uxbridge today. *Author's collection*

The implementation of these plans began in earnest in 1938 and the first train of Pre-1938 Tube Stock ran on the Central Line on 15 November 1938. Train lengths were initially six cars maximum because of the operating restrictions at Wood Lane. The Central's non-standard current arrangements (centre third rail with return through the running rails) remained for the time being and the Pre-1938 stock had to be temporarily adapted to suit until the LT standard was commissioned in May 1940. Enough Pre-1938 Tube Stock had been transferred to the Central to enable the old CLR stock of 1900–17 vintage to be withdrawn by June 1939.

Meanwhile, the Northern City Line had been equipped with Pre-1938 Tube Stock from May 1939. This line had non-standard current arrangements (current rails outside each running rail) and had to be converted before the new trains could operate. Because the Northern City Line had hitherto 'main line' size stock, the tracks had to be raised to a 'compromise' train-platform height. This short branch continued to operate control trailers in their own right (M-CT) to which was added a further four cars (CT-T-T-M) at rush hours, making six cars per full length train (one or two five-car sets operated in the early days). The extension of the Bakerloo Line to Stanmore opened in November 1939. For crew familiarisation purposes, Pre-1938 stock began working passenger trips between Wembley Park and Stanmore from 27 March 1939 until replaced by 1938 Tube Stock from the end of July 1939.

With the imminence and subsequent outbreak of the Second World War, not all the 1935–40 New Works plans came to fruition immediately, and some, in the event, not at all. A total of 83 control trailers were converted to trailers between April 1938 and June 1940 instead of 90, and only 20 out of the 26 proposed conversions of 'A' motor cars to 'D' motors were done between May 1938 and November 1939. The proposed modifications of the future Central Line cars continued for a time, but because work on the extensions was subsequently deferred, the completed cars had to be stored. Bakerloo Line trains were not able to be increased from six- to seven-car lengths and homes had to be found for those cars that were temporarily surplus to requirements – all this and with the continued delivery of 1938 Tube Stock.

Just less than 200 cars destined for the Central Line were stored in the partly completed depot at Hainault but, as the depot was acquired by the U.S. Army Transportation Corps for the assembly of railway rolling stock concerned with wartime activities, they were soon moved into the open sidings. Cars were also stored in the open at Stanmore, Neasden, Highgate, Edgware, Golders Green and Morden and in the depots of the allocated line. Most cars were stored for the duration of the Second World War but there were some movements of vehicles in the interim. Some cars found less glamorous roles, the motor cars being ideal for engineering and pilot duties – some were repainted grey for the purpose. Some cars worked as 'Tube Refreshment Specials' (also colloquially known as 'Bun Trains') delivering food and drink to the tube stations in use as air raid shelters. Some cars saw less dignified roles as storerooms, home guard stores and ARP shelters. The constraints of wartime conditions resulted in anti-blast netting being applied to windows (of all tube stock) – a later addition was that of diamond-shaped sections of clear glass for station observation purposes. Whilst this was removed soon after hostilities ended, its remains lingered on some of the cars for many years after. Because tube cars had doors which curved up into the roof, it was difficult to conceal the interior lighting during the blackout. By the outbreak of the war tube car interiors were fitted with three 'Osglim' lamps that were attached to the battens along the car ceilings. These gave out a very dim light, which resulted in complaints. Subsequently, additional lighting was provided using the same battens but with the lighting concealed in troughs, which went some way to improve matters.

Below 1928 UCC motor car 3062 is seen at Wembley Park on a southbound Bakerloo service to Elephant & Castle, soon after the opening of through services to Stanmore. Note the E.P. lettering by the cab door, indicating electro-pneumatic braking. In the background is a Metropolitan Railway saloon stock train, that visible in the picture being of 1904 vintage with its narrow saloon windows. *Charles F. Klapper/LURS*

Above Nine-car train operation began on the Northern Line in November 1937, each train being formed of two three-car M-T-M sets with three trailers in between them. The guard rode on the seventh car, because this would always stop in the station and he can just be seen in this posed view in Golders Green depot. *LT Museum*

Below Seen at Acton Town on 16 February 1952 is a 1925 MCCW former control trailer (5295) which was one of 90 that had been converted to a trailer (by removing the driving equipment from the cab) and renumbered 75295. It was not until 1955, however, that a programme had begun to convert the disued cab area into passenger accommodation. *Alan B. Cross*

Despite many cars being damaged in air raids, no Pre-1938 Tube Stock cars had to be scrapped as a result. The only one that was written off was DM 3669 which was involved in a collision with a Metropolitan Line train in fog near Eastcote in January 1941. Otherwise the fleet remained complete.

With deliveries of sufficient 1938 Tube Stock to the Northern Line, the Pre-1938 Tube Stock in passenger service on that line was gradually transferred out. Although no exact date can be ascertained as to when the last one ran on the Northern Line, it was believed to have been in the spring of 1942 on the 'main line' service and shortly after on the Mill Hill East shuttle.

When hostilities had ceased, work resumed on the Central Line's extensions, both east and west, apart from the section between West Ruislip and Denham, which had already been abandoned because it fell in 'green belt' land. The priority was to return to passenger service all the cars stored, along with those that had served in the less glamorous roles during the war years. Whilst the cars stored in the open had superficial maintenance and minor repairs done on them, it was found that six years or so of such conditions necessitated far more work than had been envisaged. Window frames were found to be warped and the rusted doors had rubber edges that had perished. The gutter drain pipes were blocked and electrical and mechanical equipment had corroded – nothing less than a complete rewire was necessary.

The original intention was to completely rehabilitate all the stored cars of Pre-1938 Tube Stock, many of which were at Hainault. After the rehabilitation had commenced, other cars were added to the programme, including those which

A seven-car westbound Piccadilly Line train skirts around Northfields depot and approaches Boston Manor in this 1949 view. The leading car is a 1931/34 motor car built by Metropolitan Cammell. *J.H. Aston*

To the casual observer, the differences between the 1931 and 1934 builds of motor car were negligible. One of the former batch, 3255, is seen at Acton Town. Note that the 'weak field' flag switch is raised, underneath the train set number. *F.G. Reynolds*

had been pilot motors and those on Tube Refreshment Specials. Although a total of 340 cars has been documented as being rehabilitated, the additional Pre-1938 Tube Stock cars that required similar treatment made that figure academic, though most of those cars involved can be identified.

By the late spring of 1946, the rehabilitation work was well under way, the first trains re-entering service in August 1946. It took until the autumn of 1948, however, to complete the programme, with some cars being returned to Hainault for short-term storage under cover until the extensions were ready. Work also resumed on the programme of equipment modification of those trains not treated, whilst the outstanding seven control trailers were converted to trailers between 1947 and 1949, making the 90 as originally intended. Six other motor cars were converted from 'A' end to 'D' end between 1948 and 1951, but not from those originally earmarked.

It was planned that the Pre-1938 Tube Stock would operate in eight-car formation on the Central Line and in anticipation, the stations were so lengthened by the beginning of the war. However, until new facilities at White City/Wood Lane were complete, six-car operation only was possible. Some seven-car trains began running from November 1947 and eight-car trains in January 1948, but even though the trains had been rehabilitated, their reliability was far from satisfactory and a full service of eight-car trains was never achieved in the period covered in this book.

One of the six 'sample' cars in Ruislip depot after rehabilitation in 1949. *LT Museum*

It was proposed that 'passenger door control' would be fitted to the Pre-1938 Tube Stock on the Central Line and to that end cars which passed through Acton Works in 1939–40 were equipped. However, these cars went into store and it was not until October 1948 that PDC was finally introduced. Meanwhile, the number of Pre-1938 Tube Stock trains on the Bakerloo Line had been steadily declining during the war and immediately after, having been replaced by the 1938 Tube Stock, some of which had also been stored, but under cover. The lengths of Bakerloo Line trains had also been increased from six cars to seven, and as far as the Pre-1938 Tube Stock was concerned, the formation was changed to have two motor cars at the north end of the train together, rather than one in the middle, because of the lesser number of station exits at that end. In their closing days on the Bakerloo Line, these trains were used only in the peaks, until the last was transferred away in May 1949.

In the late 1940s, consideration was being given to relocating train guards in the middle of trains. This would reduce the operative number of equipment panels to be provided (up to four on an eight-car train) and would enable the guard to undertake other functions not possible by being at the rear. One Piccadilly Line train was thus modified, middle DM 3055 being fitted with the additional equipment. It entered service on 29 January 1951 but was withdrawn in July, the disadvantages outweighing the advantages.

Visible changes to the stock occurred from 1952 when the cream colour around the saloon windows was abandoned in favour of all-red, while soon after, the 'LONDON TRANSPORT' transfers were omitted from all but driving motor cars.

With the large reorganisation of the tube fleets in the 1950–53 period connected with the 1938–49 Tube Stock, the earlier examples of Pre-1938 Tube Stock

(1923–27) worked on the Central and Northern City lines, while the later breeds (1927–34) worked on the Piccadilly. There were, however, some exceptions with some UCC cars on the Central, along with the 1930 'Watford Replacement' batch. Following this reorganisation, a number of Pre-1938 cars were surplus to requirements, comprising 14 motor cars and 39 trailers. A programme was begun to convert the motor cars into Ballast Motors to replace the Gate Stock Ballast Motors of 1906–07 vintage that were so converted in 1930. The new conversion comprised four 1923 Cammell Laird cars and ten 1923 MCCW cars, the later including motor car 3500 which was involved in the Stratford collision of 8 April 1953. The first conversions were completed during 1954, the others in 1955 and all were finished in service stock grey livery

Of the 39 trailers withdrawn, 20 were those control trailers converted to trailers (leaving 70 of them in service), five 'sample' trailer cars of 1922 and two damaged 1930 MCCW trailers. The balance of 12 cars were all of 1923 vintage built by Cammell Laird and Birmingham. All but two were scrapped in 1954 with the remaining two converted to Rail Grinding Cars in 1956.

Although ultimately the Pre-1938 fleet was regarded as 'standard' stock, there remained two types, according to their battery type – 12 volt or 50 volt trains, on the Central and Piccadilly lines respectively, an anomaly which remained until their demise.

Further conversions of Pre-1938 driving motor cars from 'D'-end to 'A'-end took place in 1957. This was as a result of the arrival of the 1956 Prototype Tube Stock on the Piccadilly Line. These three new trains enabled a small number of Pre-1938 cars to be transferred to the Central Line, making up more eight-car trains. The Central Line, however, required more 'A' cars, hence the conversion of four cars from 'D' to 'A', of which three (3775, 3779 and 3783) were originally 'A'-end cars and once again acquired their former numbers (3372, 3044 and 3296 respectively).

Interior of 'sample' trailer 7273 in rehabilitated condition. This was one of 37 cars of Pre-1938 Tube Stock that were scrapped in 1954. *LT Museum*

It will be recalled that 90 control trailers were converted to trailers between 1938 and 1949, having the cab equipment removed. Their car numbers were prefixed '7' to become 75xxx. Of these, 20 were scrapped in 1954 following the reorganisation of the tube stock fleet in the early-1950s. It was, however, decided to make the disused cab areas of the remaining cars available to the public and to that end a trial conversion was undertaken at Acton Works on 75303 in early-1954. Two pairs of longitudinal seats were installed in the former cab. Although the cab doors were removed, the bulkheads remained albeit with windows inserted. Not surprisingly, perhaps, being out of the way at the car ends, these four extra seats became known as "lovers' seats". The conversion of the other 69 cars then followed through to early-1958 and one other control trailer car (5155) was converted at the end of the programme, making a total of 71 in all.

To increase the three two-car units of 1935 Tube Stock to three cars on the Central Line shuttle services, three 1927 MCCW cars were converted at Acton Works in 1958 to run with the newer motor car pairs.

The Pre-1938 Tube Stock fleet was reduced by a further five cars that were written off in 1958–59.

In the lists that follow, cars are shown in their 1930s numbers, in type and numerical order, subdivided by the various batches constructed by the various car builders. Conversions and renumberings are shown after the initial list but such cars are identified thus * in these lists. It should be remembered that some cars were not renumbered until after the formation of the LPTB, into 1935.

A view of a control trailer converted to a trailer, but after the addition of seats in the former driver's compartment, undertaken in 1954–58.
LT Museum

DRIVING MOTOR CARS – 645

1929 HAMPSTEAD ADDITIONAL STOCK
BUILT BY U.C.C. – Total 18

Orig. No.	1930s No.	Orig. No.	1930s No.	Orig. No.	1930s No.	Orig. No.	1930s No.	Orig. No.	1930s No.
188	3000	192	3004	196	3008	200	3012	204	3016
187	3001	191	3005	195	3009	199	3013	203	3017
190	3002	194	3006	198	3010	202	3014		
189	3003	193	3007	197	3011	201	3015		

1928 FRENCH AIR-DOOR REPLACEMENT
BUILT BY U.C.C. – Total 20

Orig. No.	1930s No.	Orig. No.	1930s No.	Orig. No.	1930s No.	Orig. No.	1930s No.	Orig. No.	1930s No.
206	3018	210	3022	214	3026	218	3030	222	3034
205	3019	209	3023	213	3027	217	3031	221	3035
208	3020	212	3024	216	3028	220	3032	224	3036
207	3021	211	3025	215	3029	219	3033	223	3037

1928 BAKERLOO GATE STOCK REPLACEMENT
BUILT BY U.C.C. – Total 57

Orig. No.	1930s No.	Orig. No.	1930s No.	Orig. No.	1930s No.	Orig. No.	1930s No.	Orig. No.	1930s No.
226	3038	232	3044*	238	3050*	244	3056	250	3062
225	3039	231	3045	237	3051	243	3057	249	3063
228	3040	234	3046	240	3052*	246	3058*	252	3064
227	3041	233	3047	239	3053	245	3059	251	3065
230	3042	236	3048	242	3054	248	3060	253	3067
229	3043	235	3049	241	3055	247	3061		

Note that the remaining 28 cars are continued in the number series 3284–3311 below.

1930 PICCADILLY EXPERIMENTAL STOCK
BUILT BY U.C.C. – Total 2

Orig. No.	1930s No.
184	3068
183	3069

1931 PICCADILLY EXTENSION STOCK
BUILT BY METROPOLITAN-CAMMELL – Total 145

All cars entered service on the Piccadilly Line apart from those noted †

Delivered	Entered service	No.	Delivered	Entered service	No.	Delivered	Entered service	No.
10.11.31	30.08.32	3070	17.02.32	29.02.32†	3119	27.04.32	26.06.33	3189
10.11.31	30.08.32	3071	15.03.32	06.06.32	3120	27.04.32	19.09.32	3191
03.12.31	31.08.32	3072	17.02.32	31.08.32	3121	27.04.32	19.09.32	3193
03.12.31	31.08.32	3073	17.03.32	09.01.33	3122	27.04.32	06.10.32	3195
03.12.31	06.10.32	3074	03.03.32	09.01.33	3123	04.05.32	16.06.33	3197
03.12.31	21.09.32	3075	24.03.32	16.06.32†	3124	04.05.32	12.09.32	3199
09.12.31	08.02.32†	3076	03.03.32	29.06.33	3125	04.05.32	30.08.32	3201
09.12.31	15.09.32	3077	14.04.32	28.04.32	3126	04.05.32	18.09.32	3203
09.12.31	15.09.32	3078	03.03.32	26.05.32†	3127	11.05.32	02.06.32	3205
09.12.31	18.09.32	3079	20.04.32	09.01.33	3128	11.05.32	20.03.33	3207
09.12.31	17.03.33	3080	03.03.32	31.08.32	3129	11.05.32	13.03.33	3209
09.12.31	12.02.32†	3081	27.04.32	09.05.32	3130	11.05.32	11.01.33	3211
15.12.31	31.08.32	3082	09.03.32	09.01.33	3131	26.05.32	29.06.32†	3213
15.12.31	09.01.33	3083	04.05.32	18.09.32	3132	26.05.32	22.06.32	3215
15.12.31	04.02.32	3084	09.03.32	13.06.32	3133	26.05.32	06.07.32†	3217
15.12.31	04.02.32	3085	11.05.32	02.06.32	3134	26.05.32	05.01.33	3219
23.12.31	12.09.32	3086	09.03.32	09.01.33	3135	26.05.32	29.06.32†	3221
23.12.31	08.02.32†	3087	01.06.32	05.01.33	3136	01.06.32	05.01.33	3223
23.12.31	08.02.32†	3088	09.03.32	02.06.33	3137	01.06.32	09.01.33	3225
23.12.31	08.02.32†	3089	08.06.32	09.01.33	3138	01.06.32	29.09.32	3227
08.01.32	10.02.32†	3090	15.03.32	22.09.32	3139	01.06.32	29.09.32	3229
08.01.32	22.02.32†	3091	15.06.32	19.09.32	3140	08.06.32	13.10.32	3231
08.01.32	17.02.32†	3092	15.03.32	18.09.32	3141	08.06.32	10.10.32	3233
08.01.32	15.02.32†	3093	21.06.32	30.09.32	3142	08.06.32	24.09.32	3235
14.01.32	18.03.32	3094	15.03.32	09.01.33	3143	08.06.32	06.10.32	3237
14.01.32	08.02.32†	3095	13.07.32	28.12.32	3144	15.06.32	13.03.33	3239
14.01.32	15.02.32†	3096	15.03.32	18.09.32	3145	15.06.32	30.09.32	3241
14.01.32	29.02.32†	3097	13.07.32	19.09.32	3146	15.06.32	19.09.32	3243
21.01.32	18.02.32	3098	17.03.32	09.01.33	3147	15.06.32	19.09.32	3245
21.01.32	13.02.32	3099	17.03.32	16.03.33	3149	21.06.32	19.09.32	3247
21.01.32	07.04.32†	3100	17.03.32	18.09.32	3151	21.06.32	09.03.33	3249
21.01.32	08.02.32†	3101	17.03.32	09.03.33	3153	21.06.32	30.09.32	3251
28.01.32	12.02.32	3102	24.03.32	09.01.33	3155	21.06.32	20.09.32	3253
28.01.32	12.02.32	3103	24.03.32	16.06.32†	3157	29.06.32	31.08.32	3255
28.01.32	15.02.32†	3104	24.03.32	18.09.32	3159	29.06.32	17.07.32†	3257
28.01.32	15.02.32†	3105	24.03.32	30.06.33	3161	29.06.32	17.07.32†	3259
02.02.32	18.03.32	3106	08.04.32	31.08.32	3163	29.06.32	19.09.32	3261
02.02.32	22.02.32†	3107	08.04.32	15.06.33	3165	29.06.32	31.08.32	3263
02.02.32	29.02.32†	3108	08.04.32	18.09.32	3167	06.07.32	18.09.32	3265
02.02.32	29.02.32†	3109	08.04.32	28.04.32	3169	06.07.32	18.09.32	3267
09.02.32	29.02.32†	3110	08.04.32	30.06.33	3171	06.07.32	24.03.33	3269
09.02.32	29.02.32†	3111	14.04.32	17.03.33	3173	06.07.32	20.09.32	3271
09.02.32	29.02.32†	3112	14.04.32	18.09.32	3175	06.07.32	19.09.32	3273
09.02.32	18.03.32	3113	14.04.32	09.01.33	3177	13.07.32	09.01.33	3275
17.02.32	09.01.33	3114	14.04.32	09.01.33	3179	13.07.32	25.04.33	3277
17.02.32	07.04.32†	3115	20.04.32	19.05.32	3181	13.07.32	19.09.32	3279
03.03.32	07.04.32†	3116	20.04.32	17.06.33	3183	13.07.32	19.09.32	3281
17.02.32	29.02.32†	3117	20.04.32	09.01.33	3185			
09.03.32	29.02.32	3118	20.04.32	17.03.33	3187			

† First entered service on District Railway shuttle services.

1928 BAKERLOO GATE STOCK REPLACEMENT
BUILT BY U.C.C. – Continued from series 3038–3067

Orig. No.	1930s No.	Orig. No.	1930s No.	Orig. No.	1930s No.	Orig. No.	1930s No.	Orig. No.	1930s No.
254	3284	260	3290	266	3296*	272	3302*	278	3308
255	3285	261	3291	267	3297	273	3303	279	3309
256	3286	262	3292	268	3298*	274	3304	280	3310*
257	3287	263	3293	269	3299	275	3305	281	3311
258	3288	264	3294	270	3300*	276	3306*		
259	3289	265	3295	271	3301	277	3307		

1927 PICCADILLY GATE STOCK REPLACEMENT
BUILT BY METRO-CARRIAGE – Total 47

Orig. No.	1930s No.	Orig. No.	1930s No.	Orig. No.	1930s No.	Orig. No.	1930s No.	Orig. No.	1930s No.
282	3312*	288	3318*	294	3324*	300	3330*	306	3336*
283	3313	289	3319	295	3325	301	3331	307	3337
284	3314	290	3320*	296	3326*	302	3332	308	3338*
285	3315	291	3321	297	3327	303	3333	309	3339
286	3316*	292	3322*	298	3328*	304	3334*	310	3340
287	3317	293	3323	299	3329	305	3335	311	3341

Note that the remaining 17 cars are continued in the number series 3364–3380 below.

1930 WATFORD (BAKERLOO) REPLACEMENT STOCK
BUILT BY METROPOLITAN-CAMMELL – Total 22

Orig. No.	1930s No.	Orig. No.	1930s No.	Orig. No.	1930s No.	Orig. No.	1930s No.	Orig. No.	1930s No.
162	3342	167	3347	172	3352*	177	3357	182	3362
163	3343	168	3348	173	3353	178	3358	161	3363
164	3344	169	3349	174	3354	179	3359		
165	3345	170	3350	175	3355	180	3360		
166	3346	171	3351	176	3356	181	3361		

1927 PICCADILLY GATE STOCK REPLACEMENT
BUILT BY METRO-CARRIAGE – Continued from series 3312–3341

Orig. No.	1930s No.	Orig. No.	1930s No.	Orig. No.	1930s No.	Orig. No.	1930s No.	Orig. No.	1930s No.
314	3364	318	3368	322	3372*	326	3376	312	3380
315	3365	319	3369	323	3373	327	3377		
316	3366	320	3370	324	3374	328	3378		
317	3367	321	3371	325	3375	313	3379		

1927 HAMPSTEAD GATE STOCK REPLACEMENT
BUILT BY METRO-CARRIAGE – Total 63

Orig. No.	1930s No.	Orig. No.	1930s No.	Orig. No.	1930s No.	Orig. No.	1930s No.	Orig. No.	1930s No.
331	3381	344	3394*	357	3407	370	3420	383	3433
332	3382	345	3395	358	3408	371	3421*	384	3434
333	3383	346	3396	359	3409	372	3422	385	3435
334	3384	347	3397	360	3410	373	3423	386	3436
335	3385	348	3398	361	3411	374	3424	387	3437
336	3386	349	3399	362	3412	375	3425	388	3438*
337	3387	350	3400	363	3413	376	3426	389	3439
338	3388	351	3401	364	3414	377	3427	390	3440
339	3389	352	3402	365	3415	378	3428	391	3441
340	3390	353	3403	366	3416	379	3429	330	3442
341	3391	354	3404	367	3417	380	3430	329	3443
342	3392	355	3405	368	3418	381	3431		
343	3393	356	3406	369	3419	382	3432*		

1923 C&SLR REPLACEMENT AND EDGWARE EXTENSION STOCK
BUILT BY CAMMELL LAIRD – Total 41

Orig. No.	1930s No.	Orig. No.	1930s No.	Orig. No.	1930s No.	Orig. No.	1930s No.	Orig. No.	1930s No.
540	3444	513	3453*	522	3462	531	3471	500	3480
539	3445	514	3454	523	3463*	532	3472	501	3481
506	3446	515	3455	524	3464	533	3473	502	3482
507	3447	516	3456	525	3465	534	3474	505	3483
508	3448	517	3457	526	3466	535	3475	504	3484
509	3449	518	3458	527	3467	536	3476*		
510	3450	519	3459	528	3468	537	3477		
511	3451	520	3460	529	3469	538	3478		
512	3452*	521	3461	530	3470	503	3479		

1923 C&SLR REPLACEMENT AND EDGWARE EXTENSION STOCK
BUILT BY METRO-CARRIAGE – Total 40

Orig. No.	1930s No.	Orig. No.	1930s No.	Orig. No.	1930s No.	Orig. No.	1930s No.	Orig. No.	1930s No.
545	3485	553	3493	561	3501*	569	3509	577	3517*
546	3486	554	3494*	562	3502	570	3510	578	3518
547	3487	555	3495	563	3503	571	3511	579	3519
548	3488	556	3496*	564	3504	572	3512	580	3520
549	3489	557	3497	565	3505*	573	3513*	541	3521
550	3490	558	3498*	566	3506*	574	3514†	542	3522
551	3491	559	3499	567	3507*	575	3515	543	3523
552	3492	560	3500*	568	3508	576	3516	544	3524

† Disposal date 5.11.59

1924 KENNINGTON & MORDEN EXTENSION STOCK
BUILT BY METRO-CARRIAGE – Total 52

Note that 3525–3531 had MV equipment, all others GEC equipment.

Orig. No.	1930s No.	Orig. No.	1930s No.	Orig. No.	1930s No.	Orig. No.	1930s No.	Orig. No.	1930s No.
585	3525	596	3536	607	3547	618	3558	629	3569
586	3526	597	3537†	608	3548	619	3559	630	3570
587	3527	598	3538	609	3549	620	3560	631	3571
582	3528	599	3539	610	3550	621	3561	632	3572
581	3529	600	3540	611	3551	622	3562	589	3573
584	3530	601	3541	612	3552	623	3563	588	3574
583	3531	602	3542	613	3553	624	3564	591	3575
592	3532	603	3543	614	3554	625	3565	590	3576
593	3533	604	3544	615	3555	626	3566		
594	3534	605	3545	616	3556	627	3567		
595	3535	606	3546	617	3557	628	3568		

† Disposal date 5.11.59

1925 KENNINGTON & MORDEN ADDITIONAL STOCK
BUILT BY CAMMELL LAIRD – Total 15

Orig. No.	1930s No.	Orig. No.	1930s No.	Orig. No.	1930s No.	Orig. No.	1930s No.
637	3577	640	3580	643	3583	646	3586
638	3578	641	3581	644	3584	647	3587
639	3579	642	3582	645	3585		

Note that the remaining 4 cars are continued in the number series 3621–3624 below.

1925 HAMPSTEAD ADDITIONAL STOCK & CLR AIR-DOOR CONVERSION COVERS
BUILT BY CAMMELL LAIRD – Total 33

Orig. No.	1930s No.	Orig. No.	1930s No.	Orig. No.	1930s No.	Orig. No.	1930s No.	Orig. No.	1930s No.
648	3588	655	3595	662	3602	669	3609	676	3616
649	3589	656	3596	663	3603	670	3610	677	3617
650	3590	657	3597	664	3604	671	3611	678	3618
651	3591	658	3598	665	3605†	672	3612	679	3619
652	3592	659	3599	666	3606	673	3613	680	3620
653	3593	660	3600	667	3607	674	3614		
654	3594	661	3601	668	3608	675	3615		

† Disposal date 23.10.59

1925 KENNINGTON & MORDEN ADDITIONAL STOCK
BUILT BY CAMMELL LAIRD – Continued from series 3577–3587

Orig. No.	1930s No.	Orig. No.	1930s No.	Orig. No.	1930s No.	Orig. No.	1930s No.
635	3621	636	3622	633	3623	634	3624

1926 HAMPSTEAD ADDITIONAL STOCK
BUILT BY METRO-CARRIAGE – Total 64

Orig. No.	1930s No.	Orig. No.	1930s No.	Orig. No.	1930s No.	Orig. No.	1930s No.
685	3625	701	3641	717	3657	733	3673
686	3626	702	3642	718	3658	734	3674
687	3627	703	3643	719	3659	735	3675
688	3628	704	3644	720	3660	736	3676
689	3629	705	3645	721	3661	737	3677
690	3630	706	3646	722	3662	738	3678‡
691	3631	707	3647	723	3663	739	3679
692	3632	708	3648	724	3664	740	3680
693	3633	709	3649	725	3665	741	3681
694	3634	710	3650	726	3666	742	3682
695	3635	711	3651	727	3667	743	3683
696	3636	712	3652	728	3668	744	3684
697	3637	713	3653	729	3669†	681	3685
698	3638	714	3654	730	3670	682	3686
699	3639	715	3655	731	3671	683	3687
700	3640	716	3656	732	3672	684	3688

† Disposal date 17.04.41
‡ Disposal date 5.11.59

1934 PICCADILLY ADDITIONAL STOCK
BUILT BY METROPOLITAN-CAMMELL – Total 26

All cars entered service on the Piccadilly Line

Delivered	Entered service	No.	Delivered	Entered service	No.	Delivered	Entered service	No.
15.10.34	29.11.34	3689	11.12.34	16.01.35	3698	11.12.34	17.01.35	3707
15.10.34	29.11.34	3690	20.11.34	31.12.34	3699	24.12.34	31.01.35	3709
15.10.34	29.11.34	3691	24.12.34	14.02.35	3700	24.12.34	18.02.35	3711
29.10.34	13.12.34	3692	26.11.34	08.01.35	3701	14.01.35	15.03.35	3713
29.10.34	11.12.34	3693	14.01.35	04.04.35	3702	14.01.35	15.03.35	3715
20.11.34	20.12.34	3694	26.11.34	05.01.35	3703	21.01.35	05.04.35	3717
29.10.34	11.12.34	3695	21.01.35	23.09.35	3704	21.01.35	06.04.35	3719
26.11.34	17.01.35	3696	11.12.34	18.01.35	3705	18.02.35	08.05.35	3721
20.11.34	20.12.34	3697	18.02.35	01.06.35	3706			

SUMMARY OF DRIVING MOTOR CARS RENUMBERED:

Reno. To	Prev. No.	Conv. date	Reno. To	Prev. No.	Conv. date.	Reno. To	Prev. No.	Conv. date
3723	3298	04.04.39	3741	3322	22.08.38	3763	3050	11.11.48
3725	3300	29.04.39	3743	3324	27.06.38	3765	3052	18.11.39
3727	3302	04.05.38	3745	3326	20.05.39	3771	3058	18.03.39
3729	3306	25.07.38	3747	3328	31.10.38	3775†	3372	11.11.48
3731	3310	11.07.38	3749	3330	25.07.38	3777	3432	21.12.48
3733	3312	15.04.39	3751	3334	17.10.38	3779†	3044	21.04.50
3735	3316	25.04.38	3753	3336	10.05.38	3781	3352	15.08.50
3737	3318	15.06.38	3755	3338	15.06.38	3783†	3296	09.02.51
3739	3320	02.05.38	3757	3438	08.04.39	3784	3421	01.02.57

† 3775, 3779 and 3783 re-converted from 'D' to 'A' end on 14.05.57, 06.06.57 and 15.08.57 respectively.

BALLAST MOTOR CAR CONVERSIONS:

Reno. To	Prev. No.	Conv. date	Reno. To	Prev. No.	Conv. date.	Reno. To	Prev. No.	Conv. date
L62	3452	02.09.54	L67	3501	19.01.55	L72	3498	**21.09.54**
L63	3463	15.07.54	L68	3494	12.10.54	L73	3513	**18.05.54**
L64	3500	07.03.55	L69	3505	21.09.54	L74	3506	**18.05.54**
L65	3453	02.09.54	L70	3496	15.06.54	L75	3517	**28.10.54**
L66	3476	18.03.54	L71	3507	08.04.54			

CONTROL TRAILERS – 270

1928 BAKERLOO GATE STOCK REPLACEMENT
BUILT BY U.C.C. – Total 68

Orig. No.	1930s No.	Orig. No.	1930s No.	Orig. No.	1930s No.	Orig. No.	1930s No.	Orig. No.	1930s No.
1974	**5000**	1985	**5022**	1996	**5044**	2007	**5066**	2018	**5088**
1975	**5002***	1986	**5024**	1997	**5046***	2008	**5068**	2019	**5090**
1976	**5004**	1987	**5026**	1998	**5048**	2009	**5070**	2020	**5092**
1977	**5006**	1988	**5028**	1999	**5050**	2010	**5072**	2021	**5094**
1978	**5008**	1989	**5030**	2000	**5052**	2011	**5074**	2022	**5096**
1979	**5010**	1990	**5032**	2001	**5054**	2012	**5076**	2023	**5098**
1980	**5012**	1991	**5034**	2002	**5056**	2013	**5078**	2024	**5100**
1981	**5014**	1992	**5036**	2003	**5058**	2014	**5080**		
1982	**5016**	1993	**5038**	2004	**5060**	2015	**5082**		
1983	**5018**	1994	**5040**	2005	**5062**	2016	**5084**		
1984	**5020**	1995	**5042**	2006	**5064**	2017	**5086**		

Note that the remaining 17 cars are continued in the number series 5153–5169 below.

1929 HAMPSTEAD ADDITIONAL STOCK
BUILT BY U.C.C. – Total 18

Orig. No.	1930s No.	Orig. No.	1930s No.	Orig. No.	1930s No.	Orig. No.	1930s No.	Orig. No.	1930s No.
2025	**5102**	2029	**5110**	2033	**5118**	2037	**5126**	2041	**5134**
2026	**5104**	2030	**5112**	2034	**5120**	2038	**5128***	2042	**5136**
2027	**5106**	2031	**5114**	2035	**5122**	2039	**5130**		
2028	**5108**	2032	**5116**	2036	**5124**	2040	**5132**		

1927 PICCADILLY GATE STOCK REPLACEMENT
BUILT BY METRO-CARRIAGE – Total 36

Orig. No.	1930s No.	Orig. No.	1930s No.	Orig. No.	1930s No.	Orig. No.	1930s No.	Orig. No.	1930s No.
1921	**5137**	1945	**5141**	1948	**5144**	1951	**5147**	1954	**5150***
1922	**5138***	1946	**5142***	1949	**5145**	1952	**5148**	1955	**5151**
1944	**5140***	1947	**5143**	1950	**5146**	1953	**5149**	1956	**5152**

1928 BAKERLOO GATE STOCK REPLACEMENT
BUILT BY U.C.C. – Continued from series 5000–5100

Orig. No.	1930s No.	Orig. No.	1930s No.	Orig. No.	1930s No.	Orig. No.	1930s No.	Orig. No.	1930s No.
1957	5153	1961	5157*	1965	5161*	1969	5165*	1973	5169*
1958	5154*	1962	5158*	1966	5162	1970	5166*		
1959	5155*	1963	5159*	1967	5163*	1971	5167*		
1960	5156*	1964	5160*	1968	5164*	1972	5168*		

1930 WATFORD (BAKERLOO) REPLACEMENT STOCK
BUILT BY METROPOLITAN-CAMMELL – Total 20

Orig. No.	1930s No.	Orig. No.	1930s No.	Orig. No.	1930s No.	Orig. No.	1930s No.	Orig. No.	1930s No.
2064	5190*	2068	5194*	2072	5198*	2076	5202	2080	5206
2063	5191	2067	5195	2071	5199	2075	5203	2079	5207
2066	5192*	2070	5196*	2074	5200	2078	5204	2082	5208
2065	5193	2069	5197	2073	5201	2077	5205	2081	5209

1923 C&SLR REPLACEMENT AND EDGWARE EXTENSION STOCK
BUILT BY METRO-CARRIAGE – Total 35

Orig. No.	1926 Reno.	1930s No.	Disposal	Orig. No.	1926 Reno.	1930s No.	Disposal
722	1722	5210		740	1740	5228	
721	1721	5211*	06.05.54	739	1739	5229*	25.06.54
724	1724	5212		742	1742	5230	
723	1723	5213*	12.07.54	741	1741	5231*	18.06.54
726	1726	5214		744	1744	5232	
725	1725	5215*	29.03.54	743	1743	5233*	09.06.54
728	1728	5216*	07.07.54	746	1746	5234	
727	1727	5217*	20.04.54	745	1745	5235*	20.04.54
730	1730	5218		748	1748	5236	
729	1729	5219*	15.06.54	747	1747	5237*	18.06.54
732	1732	5220		750	1750	5238	
731	1731	5221*	26.05.54	749	1749	5239*	03.08.54
734	1734	5222		752	1752	5240	
733	1733	5223*	20.05.54	751	1751	5241*	
736	1736	5224		754	1754	5242	
735	1735	5225*	20.05.54	753	1753	5243*	01.09.54
738	1738	5226		755	1755	5245*	
737	1737	5227*	30.04.54				

1924 KENNINGTON & MORDEN EXTENSION STOCK
BUILT BY CAMMELL LAIRD – Total 25

Orig. No.	1930s No.	Orig. No.	1930s No.	Orig. No.	1930s No.	Orig. No.	1930s No.	Orig. No.	1930s No.
1756	5246	1761	5251*	1766	5256	1771	5261*	1776	5266
1757	5247*	1762	5252	1767	5257	1772	5262	1777	5267*
1758	5248	1763	5253*	1768	5258	1773	5263*	1778	5268
1759	5249*	1764	5254	1769	5259*	1774	5264	1779	5269*
1760	5250	1765	5255*	1770	5260	1775	5265*	1780	5270

1922 'COMPETITION' STOCK
BUILT BY GLOUCESTER – Total 1

Orig. No.	1924 Reno.	1926 Reno.	1930s No.	Disposal
720	781	1781	5271*	19.03.54

1925 KENNINGTON & MORDEN ADDITIONAL STOCK
BUILT BY METRO-CARRIAGE – Total 27

Orig. No.	1930s No.	Orig. No.	1930s No.	Orig. No.	1930s No.	Orig. No.	1930s No.	Orig. No.	1930s No.
1782	5272	1788	5278	1794	5284	1800	5290	1806	5296
1783	5273	1789	5279	1795	5285	1801	5291	1807	5297*
1784	5274	1790	5280	1796	5286	1802	5292	1808	5298
1785	5275	1791	5281	1797	5287	1803	5293		
1786	5276	1792	5282	1798	5288	1804	5294		
1787	5277	1793	5283	1799	5289	1805	5295*		

1925 HAMPSTEAD ADDITIONAL STOCK & CLR AIR-DOOR CONVERSION COVERS
BUILT BY METRO-CARRIAGE – Total 40

Orig. No.	1930s No.	Orig. No.	1930s No.	Orig. No.	1930s No.	Orig. No.	1930s No.	Orig. No.	1930s No.
1809	5299*	1817	5307*	1825	5315*	1833	5323*	1841	5331*
1810	5300	1818	5308	1826	5316	1834	5324	1842	5332
1811	5301*	1819	5309*	1827	5317*	1835	5325*	1843	5333*
1812	5302	1820	5310	1828	5318	1836	5326	1844	5334
1813	5303*	1821	5311*	1829	5319*	1837	5327*	1845	5335*
1814	5304	1822	5312	1830	5320	1838	5328	1846	5336
1815	5305*	1823	5313*	1831	5321*	1839	5329*	1847	5337*
1816	5306	1824	5314	1832	5322	1840	5330	1848	5338

1927 PICCADILLY GATE STOCK REPLACEMENT
BUILT BY METRO-CARRIAGE – Continued from series 5137–5152

Orig. No.	1930s No.	Orig. No.	1930s No.	Orig. No.	1930s No.	Orig. No.	1930s No.	Orig. No.	1930s No.
1923	5339*	1928	5344	1933	5349*	1938	5354	1943	5359*
1924	5340	1929	5345*	1934	5350	1939	5355*		
1925	5341*	1930	5346	1935	5351*	1940	5356		
1926	5342	1931	5347*	1936	5352	1941	5357*		
1927	5343*	1932	5348	1937	5353*	1942	5358		

CONTROL TRAILER CAR TURNED AND RENUMBERED:

Reno. To.	Prev. No.	Date
5013	5046	16.02.35

CONTROL TRAILER CARS CONVERTED TO TRAILERS AND RENUMBERED:

Reno. To	Prev. No.	Date	Reno. To	Prev. No.	Date.	Reno. To	Prev. No.	Date
75002	5002	09.09.39	75219	5219	21.11.38	75301	5301	09.12.39
75013	5013	07.09.39	75217	5217	24.06.39	75303	5303	09.03.40
75128	5128	11.02.39	75221	5221	02.03.40	75305	5305	11.11.39
75138	5138	18.05.38	75223	5223	14.04.38	75307	5307	30.03.40
75140	5140	31.05.38	75225	5225	30.03.40	75309	5309	06.01.48
75142	5142	25.04.38	75227	5227	04.05.40	75311	5311	02.12.39
75150	5150	01.07.39	75229	5229	13.10.47	75313	5313	11.11.39
75154	5154	01.07.39	75231	5231	09.01.39	75315	5315	27.06.38
75155	5155	17.04.58	75233	5233	03.02.40	75317	5317	14.06.47
75156	5156	23.09.39	75235	5235	22.06.40	75319	5319	11.11.39
75157	5157	14.09.38	75237	5237	17.02.40	75321	5321	20.04.40
75158	5158	16.09.39	75239	5239	16.12.39	75323	5323	27.01.40
75159	5159	16.12.39	75241	5241	18.11.39	75325	5325	10.02.40
75160	5160	28.10.39	75243	5243	16.12.39	75327	5327	09.12.39
75161	5161	04.10.38	75245	5245	02.01.39	75329	5329	02.05.38
75163	5163	07.05.47	75247	5247	16.03.40	75331	5331	20.01.40
75164	5164	25.03.39	75249	5249	13.04.40	75333	5333	20.01.40
75165	5165	10.02.40	75251	5251	02.03.40	75335	5335	03.08.38
75166	5166	29.08.38	75253	5253	06.02.48	75337	5337	11.11.39
75167	5167	09.01.39	75255	5255	18.11.39	75339	5339	20.01.40
75168	5168	18.02.39	75259	5259	10.02.40	75341	5341	09.11.38
75169	5169	25.11.39	75261	5261	20.04.40	75343	5343	29.06.38
75190	5190	09.01.39	75263	5263	02.03.40	75345	5345	09.11.38
75192	5192	11.07.38	75265	5265	08.06.40	75347	5347	22.08.38
75194	5194	09.09.39	75267	5267	21.10.39	75349	5349	09.11.38
75196	5196	02.12.39	75269	5269	25.09.47	75351	5351	03.08.38
75198	5198	28.08.39	75271	5271	11.07.38	75353	5353	22.08.38
75211	5211	15.07.38	75295	5295	20.04.40	75355	5355	29.08.38
75213	5213	13.01.40	75297	5297	25.05.40	75357	5357	02.01.39
75215	5215	17.02.40	75299	5299	25.11.39	75359	5359	22.04.39
75216	5216	07.10.49						

RAIL GRINDING CAR CONVERSIONS:

Reno. To	Prev. No.	Conv. date	Reno. To	Prev. No.	Conv. date.
RG802	75241	04.09.56	RG803	75245	04.09.56

TRAILERS – 551

1927 PICCADILLY GATE STOCK REPLACEMENT
BUILT BY METRO-CARRIAGE – Total 53

Orig. No.	1930s No.	Orig. No.	1930s No.	Orig. No.	1930s No.	Orig. No.	1930s No.	Orig. No.	1930s No.
1245	7000	1249	7004	1253	7008	1257	7012	1261	7016
1246	7001	1250	7005	1254	7009	1258	7013		
1247	7002	1251	7006	1255	7010	1259	7014		
1248	7003	1252	7007	1256	7011	1260	7015		

Note that the remaining 36 cars are continued in the number series 7190–7214 and 7559–7569 below.

1928 BAKERLOO GATE STOCK REPLACEMENT
BUILT BY U.C.C. – Total 37

Orig. No.	1930s No.	Orig. No.	1930s No.	Orig. No.	1930s No.	Orig. No.	1930s No.	Orig. No.	1930s No.
1262	7017	1282	7022	1287	7027	1292	7032	1297	7037
1263	7018	1283	7023	1288	7028	1293	7033	1298	7038
1264	7019	1284	7024	1289	7029	1294	7034		
1280	7020	1285	7025	1290	7030	1295	7035		
1281	7021	1286	7026	1291	7031	1296	7036		

Note that the remaining 15 cars are continued in the number series 7215–7229 below.

1929 HAMPSTEAD ADDITIONAL STOCK
BUILT BY U.C.C. – Total 17

Orig. No.	1930s No.	Orig. No.	1930s No.	Orig. No.	1930s No.	Orig. No.	1930s No.	Orig. No.	1930s No.
1299	7039	1303	7043	1307	7047	1311	7051	1315	7055
1300	7040	1304	7044	1308	7048	1312	7052		
1301	7041	1305	7045	1309	7049	1313	7053		
1302	7042	1306	7046	1310	7050	1314	7054		

1930 PICCADILLY EXPERIMENTAL STOCK
BUILT BY U.C.C. – Total 4

Orig. No.	1930s No.	Orig. No.	1930s No.	Orig. No.	1930s No.	Orig. No.	1930s No.
1336	7056	1337	7057	1338	7058	1339	7059

1931 PICCADILLY EXTENSION STOCK
BUILT BY BIRMINGHAM – Total 90

All cars entered service on the Piccadilly Line apart from those noted †

Delivered	Entered service	No.	Delivered	Entered service	No.	Delivered	Entered service	No.
23.01.32	08.02.32†	7060	04.04.32	31.08.32	7090	23.05.32	09.01.33	7120
23.01.32	08.02.32†	7061	04.04.32	18.09.32	7091	23.05.32	01.10.32	7121
29.01.32	08.02.32†	7062	04.04.32	31.08.32	7092	23.05.32	19.09.32	7122
29.01.32	08.02.32†	7063	04.04.32	13.03.33	7093	23.05.32	29.09.32	7123
06.02.32	10.02.32†	7064	11.04.32	29.09.32	7094	30.05.32	19.09.32	7124
06.02.32	12.02.32†	7065	11.04.32	31.08.32	7095	30.05.32	19.09.32	7125
06.02.32	15.02.32†	7066	11.04.32	17.03.33	7096	30.05.32	19.09.32	7126
15.02.32	29.02.32†	7067	11.04.32	20.03.33	7097	30.05.32	09.01.33	7127
15.02.32	29.02.32†	7068	18.04.32	16.06.32†	7098	06.06.32	31.08.32	7128
15.02.32	22.02.32†	7069	18.04.32	28.04.32	7099	06.06.32	30.09.32	7129
22.02.32	29.02.32†	7070	18.04.32	16.06.32†	7100	06.06.32	12.09.32	7130
22.02.32	29.02.32†	7071	18.04.32	28.04.32	7101	06.06.32	31.08.32	7131
22.02.32	29.02.32†	7072	18.04.32	28.04.32	7102	20.06.32	02.07.32†	7132
29.02.32	07.04.32†	7073	18.04.32	28.04.32	7103	20.06.32	02.07.32†	7133
29.02.32	26.05.32†	7074	25.04.32	09.01.33	7104	20.06.32	18.09.32	7134
29.02.32	04.03.32†	7075	25.04.32	09.01.33	7105	20.06.32	18.09.32	7135
29.02.32	14.03.32†	7076	25.04.32	31.08.32	7106	20.06.32	02.07.32†	7136
07.03.32	18.03.32	7077	25.04.32	31.08.32	7107	20.06.32	02.07.32†	7137
07.03.32	18.03.32	7078	02.05.32	05.01.33	7108	30.07.32	09.01.33	7138
07.03.32	18.03.32	7079	02.05.32	05.01.33	7109	30.07.32	06.10.32	7139
14.03.32	09.01.33	7080	02.05.32	05.01.33	7110	27.06.32	17.07.32†	7140
14.03.32	09.01.33	7081	02.05.32	13.03.33	7111	27.06.32	17.07.32†	7141
14.03.32	09.01.33	7082	09.05.32	13.03.33	7112	27.06.32	19.09.32	7142
14.03.32	24.03.33	7083	09.05.32	09.01.33	7113	27.06.32	09.01.33	7143
21.03.32	09.01.33	7084	09.05.32	18.09.32	7114	17.07.32	18.09.32	7144
21.03.32	31.08.32	7085	09.05.32	18.09.32	7115	17.07.32	18.09.32	7145
21.03.32	20.09.32	7086	13.05.32	13.06.32	7116	17.07.32	30.09.32	7146
21.03.32	09.01.33	7087	13.05.32	13.06.32	7117	17.07.32	18.09.32	7147
21.03.32	18.09.32	7088	13.05.32	13.06.32	7118	30.07.32	19.09.32	7148
04.04.32	09.01.33	7089	13.05.32	13.06.32	7119	30.07.32	19.09.32	7149

† First entered service on District Railway shuttle services.

1931 PICCADILLY EXTENSION STOCK
BUILT BY GLOUCESTER – Total 40

All cars entered service on the Piccadilly Line

Delivered	Entered service	No.	Delivered	Entered service	No.	Delivered	Entered service	No.
05.03.32	18.03.32	7150	06.04.32	30.08.32	7164	13.05.32	02.06.32	7178
05.03.32	16.03.33	7151	19.04.32	09.03.33	7165	13.05.32	02.06.32	7179
05.03.32	15.09.32	7152	19.04.32	09.03.33	7166	13.05.32	02.06.32	7180
05.03.32	09.03.33	7153	19.04.32	09.01.33	7167	01.06.32	22.06.32	7181
05.03.32	15.09.32	7154	19.04.32	16.03.33	7168	01.06.32	22.06.32	7182
05.03.32	18.09.32	7155	19.04.32	09.01.33	7169	01.06.32	22.06.32	7183
19.03.32	18.09.32	7156	19.04.32	18.09.32	7170	01.06.32	22.06.32	7184
19.03.32	09.01.33	7157	03.05.32	19.09.32	7171	01.06.32	19.09.32	7185
19.03.32	09.01.33	7158	03.05.32	19.09.32	7172	17.06.32	24.03.33	7186
19.03.32	09.01.33	7159	03.05.32	12.07.32	7173	17.06.32	17.06.33	7187
06.04.32	30.09.32	7160	03.05.32	03.06.32	7174	17.06.32	19.09.32	7188
06.04.32	31.08.32	7161	03.05.32	03.06.32	7175	17.06.32	19.09.32	7189
06.04.32	30.08.32	7162	03.05.32	12.09.32	7176			
06.04.32	30.08.32	7163	13.05.32	02.06.32	7177			

1927 PICCADILLY GATE STOCK REPLACEMENT
BUILT BY METRO-CARRIAGE – Continued from series 7000–7016

Orig. No.	1930s No.	Orig. No.	1930s No.	Orig. No.	1930s No.	Orig. No.	1930s No.	Orig. No.	1930s No.
1220	7190	1225	7195	1230	7200	1235	7205	1240	7210
1221	7191	1226	7196	1231	7201	1236	7206	1241	7211
1222	7192	1227	7197	1232	7202	1237	7207	1242	7212
1223	7193	1228	7198	1233	7203	1238	7208	1243	7213
1224	7194	1229	7199	1234	7204	1239	7209	1244	7214

Note that the remaining 11 cars are continued in the number series 7559–7569 below.

1928 BAKERLOO GATE STOCK REPLACEMENT
BUILT BY U.C.C. – Continued from series 7017–7038

Orig. No.	1930s No.	Orig. No.	1930s No.	Orig. No.	1930s No.	Orig. No.	1930s No.	Orig. No.	1930s No.
1265	7215	1268	7218	1271	7221	1274	7224	1277	7227
1266	7216	1269	7219	1272	7222	1275	7225	1278	7228
1267	7217	1270	7220	1273	7223	1276	7226	1279	7229

1930 WATFORD (BAKERLOO) REPLACEMENT STOCK
BUILT BY METROPOLITAN-CAMMELL – Total 20

Orig. No.	1930s No.	Disposal	Orig. No.	1930s No.	Disposal	Orig. No.	1930s No.	Orig. No.	1930s No.
1340	7250	19.03.54	1345	7255	08.04.54	1350	7260	1355	7265
1341	7251		1346	7256		1351	7261	1356	7266
1342	7252		1347	7257		1352	7262	1357	7267
1343	7253		1348	7258		1353	7263	1358	7268
1344	7254		1349	7259		1354	7264	1359	7269

1922 'COMPETITION' STOCK – Total 5

Orig. No.	1930s No.	Built by	Disposal
820	7270	Gloucester	14.05.54
821	7271	Leeds Forge	26.05.54
822	7272	Metro-Carriage	09.06.54
823	7273	Birmingham	19.03.54
824	7274	Cammell Laird	30.04.54

1923 C&SLR REPLACEMENT AND EDGWARE EXTENSION STOCK
BUILT BY CAMMELL LAIRD – Total 40

Orig. No.	1930s No.	Disposal	Orig. No.	1930s No.	Disposal	Orig. No.	1930s No.	Disposal
825	7275		839	7289		853	7303	
826	7276		840	7290		854	7304	
827	7277		841	7291	07.07.54	855	7305	
828	7278	12.04.54	842	7292		856	7306	
829	7279		843	7293		857	7307	
830	7280		844	7294	12.04.54	858	7308	
831	7281		845	7295		859	7309	
832	7282		846	7296		860	7310	
833	7283		847	7297	25.06.54	861	7311	12.07.54
834	7284	30.03.54	848	7298		862	7312	
835	7285		849	7299		863	7313	
836	7286		850	7300		864	7314	
837	7287		851	7301				
838	7288	20.08.54	852	7302				

1923 C&SLR REPLACEMENT AND EDGWARE EXTENSION STOCK
BUILT BY BIRMINGHAM – Total 35

Orig. No.	1930s No.	Disposal	Orig. No.	1930s No.	Disposal	Orig. No.	1930s No.	Disposal
865	7315		877	7327		889	7339	08.04.54
866	7316		878	7328		890	7340	
867	7317		879	7329		891	7341	
868	7318	28.07.54	880	7330		892	7342	
869	7319	30.03.54	881	7331	14.08.54	893	7343	
870	7320		882	7332		894	7344	
871	7321		883	7333		895	7345	
872	7322	03.11.58	884	7334		896	7346	
873	7323		885	7335		897	7347	
874	7324		886	7336		898	7348	
875	7325		887	7337		899	7349	
876	7326	03.08.54	888	7338				

1924 KENNINGTON & MORDEN EXTENSION STOCK
BUILT BY BIRMINGHAM – Total 50

Orig. No.	1930s No.	Orig. No.	1930s No.	Orig. No.	1930s No.	Orig. No.	1930s No.	Orig. No.	1930s No.
900	7350	910	7360	920	7370	930	7380	940	7390
901	7351	911	7361	921	7371	931	7381	941	7391
902	7352	912	7362	922	7372	932	7382	942	7392
903	7353	913	7363	923	7373	933	7383	943	7393
904	7354	914	7364	924	7374	934	7384	944	7394
905	7355	915	7365	925	7375	935	7385	945	7395
906	7356	916	7366	926	7376	936	7386	946	7396
907	7357	917	7367	927	7377	937	7387	947	7397
908	7358	918	7368	928	7378	938	7388	948	7398
909	7359	919	7369	929	7379	939	7389	949	7399

1925 HAMPSTEAD ADDITIONAL STOCK & CLR AIR-DOOR CONVERSION COVERS
BUILT BY METRO-CARRIAGE – Total 5

Orig. No.	1930s No.	Orig. No.	1930s No.	Orig. No.	1930s No.	Orig. No.	1930s No.	Orig. No.	1930s No.
950	7400	951	7401	952	7402	953	7403	954	7404

1926 HAMPSTEAD ADDITIONAL STOCK
BUILT BY METRO-CARRIAGE – Total 48

Orig. No.	1930s No.	Orig. No.	1930s No.	Orig. No.	1930s No.	Orig. No.	1930s No.	Orig. No.	1930s No.
1055	7405	1065	7415	1075	7425	1085	7435	1095	7445
1056	7406	1066	7416	1076	7426	1086	7436	1096	7446
1057	7407	1067	7417	1077	7427	1087	7437	1097	7447
1058	7408	1068	7418	1078	7428	1088	7438	1098	7448
1059	7409	1069	7419	1079	7429	1089	7439	1099	7449
1060	7410	1070	7420	1080	7430	1090	7440	1100	7450
1061	7411	1071	7421	1081	7431	1091	7441	1101	7451
1062	7412	1072	7422	1082	7432	1092	7442	1054	7452
1063	7413	1073	7423	1083	7433	1093	7443		
1064	7414	1074	7424	1084	7434	1094	7444		

1927 HAMPSTEAD GATE STOCK REPLACEMENT
BUILT BY METRO-CARRIAGE – Total 107

Orig. No.	1930s No.	Orig. No.	1930s No.	Orig. No.	1930s No.	Orig. No.	1930s No.	Orig. No.	1930s No.
1103	7453	1125	7475	1147	7497*	1169	7519*	1191	7541*
1104	7454	1126	7476*	1148	7498*	1170	7520*	1192	7542*
1105	7455	1127	7477	1149	7499	1171	7521*	1193	7543*
1106	7456	1128	7478	1150	7500*	1172	7522*	1194	7544*
1107	7457	1129	7479	1151	7501	1173	7523*	1195	7545*
1108	7458	1130	7480*	1152	7502	1174	7524*	1196	7546*
1109	7459	1131	7481	1153	7503	1175	7525*	1197	7547*
1110	7460	1132	7482	1154	7504*	1176	7526*	1198	7548*
1111	7461	1133	7483	1155	7505	1177	7527*	1199	7549*
1112	7462	1134	7484	1156	7506*	1178	7528*	1200	7550*
1113	7463	1135	7485	1157	7507*	1179	7529*	1201	7551*
1114	7464	1136	7486	1158	7508	1180	7530*	1202	7552*
1115	7465	1137	7487	1159	7509*	1181	7531*	1203	7553*
1116	7466	1138	7488	1160	7510*	1182	7532*	1204	7554*
1117	7467	1139	7489*	1161	7511*	1183	7533*	1205	7555*
1118	7468	1140	7490	1162	7512*	1184	7534*	1206	7556*
1119	7469	1141	7491	1163	7513*	1185	7535*	1207	7557*
1120	7470	1142	7492*	1164	7514*	1186	7536*	1208	7558*
1121	7471	1143	7493	1165	7515*	1187	7537*		
1122	7472	1144	7494	1166	7516*	1188	7538*		
1123	7473	1145	7495	1167	7517*	1189	7539*		
1124	7474	1146	7496	1168	7518*	1190	7540*		

Note that the remaining one car is numbered at the end of the trailer numbering series – see below.

1927 PICCADILLY GATE STOCK REPLACEMENT
BUILT BY METRO-CARRIAGE – Continued from series 7000–7016 and 7190–7214

Orig. No.	1930s No.	Orig. No.	1930s No.	Orig. No.	1930s No.	Orig. No.	1930s No.
1209	7559*	1212	7562*	1215	7565*	1218	7568*
1210	7560*	1213	7563*	1216	7566*	1219	7569*
1211	7561*	1214	7564*	1217	7567*		

1927 HAMPSTEAD GATE STOCK REPLACEMENT
BUILT BY METRO-CARRIAGE – Continued from series 7453–7558

Orig. No.	1930s No.
1102	7570*

'58 TRAILER' CONVERSIONS AND ASSOCIATED TRAILERS RENUMBERED:

1930s No.	Reno.	Date	58 Trailer Reno.	Date	1930s No.	Reno.	Date	58 Trailer Reno.	Date
7476	7513	05.09.38	**70513**	19.12.38	7536			**70536**	16.01.39
7480	7525	02.09.38	**70525**	28.11.38	7537	**7498**	09.09.38		
7489	7526	02.09.38	**70526**	05.12.38	7538	**7500**	05.09.38		
7492	7528	29.08.38	**70528**	31.10.38	7539			**70539**	16.01.39
7497	7534	19.08.38	**70534**	14.11.38	7540			**70540**	04.07.38
7498	7537	05.09.38	**70537**	14.11.38	7541	**7504**	31.08.38		
7500	7538	16.09.38	**70538**	23.01.39	7542			**70542**	17.10.38
7504	7541	31.08.38	**70541**	23.01.39	7543	**7506**	05.09.38		
7506	7543	05.09.38	**70543**	28.11.38	7544			**70544**	10.10.38
7507	7546	02.09.38	**70546**	28.11.38	7545			**70545**	23.01.39
7509	7547	29.08.38	**70547**	05.12.38	7546	**7507**	02.09.38		
7510	7555	31.08.38	**70555**	21.11.38	7547	**7509**	29.08.38		
7512	7568	29.08.38	**70568**	24.12.38	7548			**70548**	07.11.38
7513	**7476**	05.09.38			7549			**70549**	07.11.38
7514			**70514**	24.12.38	7550			**70550**	12.12.38
7515			**70515**	04.10.38	7551			**70551**	06.02.39
7516			**70516**	21.11.38	7552			**70552**	12.12.38
7517			**70517**	05.12.38	7553			**70553**	21.11.38
7518			**70518**	16.01.39	7554			**70554**	24.10.38
7519			**70519**	31.10.38	7555	**7510**	31.08.38		
7520			**70520**	04.10.38	7556			**70556**	17.10.38
7521			**70521**	31.10.38	7557			**70557**	05.12.38
7522			**70522**	07.11.38	7558			**70558**	24.12.38
7523			**70523**	05.09.38	7559			**70559**	24.12.38
7524			**70524**	05.12.38	7560			**70560**	20.09.38
7525	**7480**	02.09.38			7561			**70561**	14.11.38
7526	**7489**	02.09.38			7562			**70562**	31.10.38
7527			**70527**	22.08.38	7563			**70563**	31.10.38
7528	**7492**	29.08.38			7564			**70564**	14.11.38
7529			**70529**	14.09.38	7565			**70565**	17.10.38
7530			**70530**	24.12.38	7566			**70566**	09.01.39
7531			**70531**	11.12.38	7567			**70567**	05.12.38
7532			**70532**	29.08.38	7568	**7512**	29.08.38		
7533			**70533**	30.01.39	7569			**70569**	28.11.38
7534	**7497**	19.08.38			7570			**70570**	21.11.38
7535			**70535**	18.05.38					

TRAILERS CONVERTED TO RUN WITH 1935 STOCK

Orig. 1930s No.	Reno. 1938	Reno. 1935 Stock	Date
7511	—	**70511**	16.06.58
7555	7510	**70510**	23.12.58
7568	7512	**70512**	08.05.58

CHAPTER FIVE

THE 1938 TUBE STOCK FAMILY

Experimental Trains

Before the last of the Pre-1938 Tube Stock had entered service (the 26 motor cars of 1934) the new LPTB was giving consideration to future rolling stock, for many additional cars would be required for extended and improved tube (and surface) lines that were to be recommended in the then forthcoming 1935–40 New Works Programme, which included re-jigged parts of some schemes proposed in the 1920s.

Most problematical was the Central Line, which had tunnels marginally smaller than the other tube lines and in 1934 a 'mock-up' was constructed at Acton Works of a 'compact' tube car. At the same time, the Morden–Edgware, Bakerloo and Piccadilly lines were having problems with line capacity and thus the question of train lengths on those lines was brought into the equation. The Morden–Edgware Line's problems were to be alleviated by the running of longer trains, but even this did not solve them, because to lengthen tube stations was extremely expensive. What was probably the 'second best' but most economical was to operate nine-car trains, with either the leading pair of cars or rear pair of cars in the tunnel at nominated tube stations. These began operation in November 1937. Time and again plans for future stock requirements changed, but the most significant in the long term was to provide new higher-capacity stock for the Morden–Edgware Line (without having to lengthen 90 platforms) and to extend 30 Central Line platforms from six- to eight-car lengths and operate the trains (Pre-1938 Tube Stock) from the Morden–Edgware Line. Another advantage would be that each line would have one type of stock. The plan was also changed so that the Bakerloo Line would operate seven-car trains instead of the eight proposed, altering again the stock requirement.

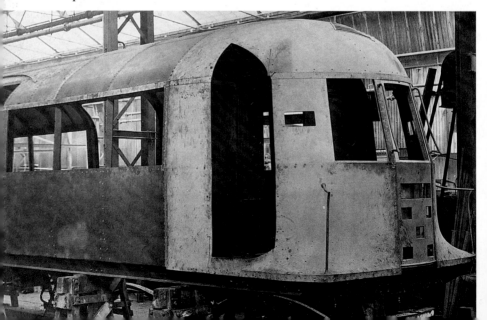

While all this was going on, the LPTB authorised in May 1935 the construction of an experimental 'high speed' six-car tube train, Metropolitan Cammell of Birmingham winning the contract. Each car was to be motored with a cab at one end of each. In keeping with the fashions of the time, the cab fronts were to be 'streamlined'. In effect their rectangular windows (the centre one incorporating the cab door) curved round, beneath which the body curved to give corner flares. The domed roof curved in line with the cab front, giving a neat front, if wasteful in space. Above the cab door on the dome, wing shaped vents were provided. The initial order for one six-car train was soon increased to four, so that GEC, BTH and Metropolitan Vickers could participate in the supply of equipment, as well as Allen West and Cromptons. The fourth train had re-designed front cab ends to eliminate the streamlined effect that was disapproved of by many. It was also thought that the coupling of streamlined cars did not look aesthetically good in the middle of trains. On this train the flat cab front gently swept upwards from each side, curving gently over the front cab door, above which was a wing-shaped ventilator.

A four-car train of 1935 Tube Stock heading westbound for Uxbridge soon after leaving North Ealing. A modification had been made to the tops of the front cab door before entering service for safety reasons. *Author's collection*

Opposite The cab end of a 1935 Tube Stock streamlined motor car under construction at the Metropolitan Cammell factory in Birmingham. The presence of the streamlined end resulted in space only for three windows in the saloon behind the cab. *Author's collection*

Interior of the first unit of 1935 Tube Stock, which did not initially have opening windows, having a system of forced ventilation. These differed from the production trains, in that the draughtscreen partitions were rather angular. *LT Museum*

The revolution with the experimental train was that all the equipment was mounted under the car floor, including the compressor. This provided more seating in the (driving motor) cars, there being no equipment compartment separating the cab and the saloon. A total of 40 seats were provided (instead of 30) on the 18 streamlined cars and, with the re-designed cab taking less space at one end, 42 on the six non-streamlined cars. In the end bays there were all longitudinal seats each side with three windows, and in the centre bay four windows with all transverse seating. Here the centre section comprised pairs of seats facing, behind which were a pair facing the back of the others. Where the doors slid back, non-opening casement windows were provided. The deep and comfortable seats were covered in moquette and the longitudinal seat spaces divided by leather armrests. On the streamlined cars the destination blind was under the window of the front cab door, beneath which were five square headlights. Because of the rounded streamlined front, two train set number positions were provided, one either side between the corner cab window and the cab door. The cream colour was carried right around the front of the train. On the flat-fronted units the train set number was located in the offside cab window, underneath which was the destination blind and beneath that the five square headlights. The flat front was painted all red. One window wiper was provided on the driver's cab window, but three, one on each side, were provided for the streamlined cars because the driver sat in the middle behind the cab door. Because the cabs also served as the guard's position (at the opposite end of the train with controls on the back wall), the cab doors extended up into the curve of the roof on all 24 cars, being hinged at the back.

The first two-car unit was delivered on 2 October 1936 with others following up to June 1937. The first flat fronted unit, the design of which had already been agreed as *the* design for the future new stock, arrived on 7 August 1937, the last on 22 October 1937.

Because the trains had equipment from four different manufacturers, all of which was experimental, and having to fit under the car floors, extensive testing was undertaken before they entered service, but a press launch took place on 17 November 1936 in Northfields depot. The trains began entering service from 8 April 1937, cautiously at first in midday off-peak service only but also in evening peak workings from 26 April 1937. The flat-fronted train began passenger service from 24 January 1938 but was transferred to the Northern Line for gauging and testing from 31 March 1938 – this design had by then been accepted for the future new stock and already had been ordered.

The flat-fronted cars of 1935 stock were also stored in the war, but were modified for use on the Central Line shuttle services. One such two-car unit is seen stabled in the siding at Loughton adjacent to the westbound line on 17 July 1952, comprising cars 10010–11010. The apparent colour difference at the tops of the doors is reflection, plus possibly a degree of wear and tear. *John H. Meredith*

The experimental cars were numbered 10000–10011 ('A' end cars) and 11000–11011 ('B' end cars – and later 'D' end cars) with the last digits being the same on each two-car unit. The flat fronted train took the last numbers 10009–10011 and 11009–11011. The intention was that units 10000–10002/11000–11002 would be equipped by Allen West/Crompton, 10003–10005/11003–11005 by GEC, 10006–10008/11006–11008 by BTH and 10009–11009/10011–11011 by MV. Before delivery in March 1936, there were changes to cars and equipment and they finished up as follows:

10000–11000	Allen West / Crompton multi-notch faceplate control
10001–11001	Allen West / Crompton straight faceplate control
10002–11002	GEC multi-notch camshaft system
10003–11003	BTH PCM control
10004–11004	GEC staggered multi-notch camshaft system
10005–11005	Allen West / Crompton straight camshaft system
10006–11006	GEC staggered multi-notch camshaft system
10007–11007	BTH PCM control
10008–11008	BTH PCM control
10009–11009	MV oil-operated power drum system
10010–11010	MV oil-operated power drum system
10011–11011	MV oil-operated power drum system

Unit 10000–11000 had no opening saloon car windows at first, with air conditioning (really forced ventilation) being provided on both cars – by J. Stone on 10000 and R. Crittall on 11000. This was unsuccessful, the equipment being removed and tilting quarter lights fitted at the usual locations. Compressors were fitted to the 10xxx cars and motor generators on the 11xxx cars. All units were operationally interchangeable but for passenger service the flat fronted units were kept together – if only for appearance sake! There were two types of centre cab doors on the streamlined cars. One had the door mounted on top and bottom rails enabling it to slide back, while on the other version the door was pivoted onto a large cast hinge, itself being pivoted to the car body below the nearside cab window. Unique to the experimental trains were the 'wing' shaped ventilators over the communicating doors and the waist level section of the draught screen at the bottom of the glass, where the dividing panels were angled at their edges.

A timetable path for a second train was available from 24 January 1938, followed by a third from 2 August 1938. A fourth followed when all units had been in service for a time, but it was rare for all four trains to be in service, with Pre-1938 Tube Stock trains often substituting. The experimental nature of the trains resulted in much of their time being spent in depots solving problems that had come to light – the learning curve was thus rather steep! The fact that the streamlined end cabs had restricted views forward did nothing to enhance their popularity. The BTH train was often 'split' to run with other streamlined units as there was a good chance that with one BTH unit, the train would reach Northfields depot without failing in service.

The proposal under the 1935–40 New Works Programme for the 1935 Tube Stock was for the three flat fronted units to be converted to two-car 'shuttle' units for the east end Central shuttle services when completed – this in fact happened, but not until 1950. The three six-car streamlined trains would each be lengthened to seven cars by the insertion of a new trailer and would remain on the Piccadilly Line, but this was one of the many plans that were thwarted by the Second World War as will be explained later.

By the autumn of 1940, all of the experimental units were taken out of service and were stored in Cockfosters depot, having taken valuable manpower to keep them going in the early years of the war. The streamlined units, however, did have an overhaul at Acton Works prior to storage. The 'official' date of storage is given as 16 May 1942 – long after the event. In the interim, proposals were put forward to improve the disliked cab layout and these changes were made on a gradual basis in 1941–42 on cars 10004 and 11004. The driving controls were moved to the conventional (left-hand, facing) position and windows either side of the cab door were extended up into the dome of the roof, enabling the driver to stand if he so wished. The intention was to run the modified motor cars at the outer ends of units 002 and 006 and operate it as a six-car block train, but the modifications were found unacceptable and the idea was abandoned. This effectively sealed their fate for return to Piccadilly Line service after the war and future plans reflected this, as will be seen. Three of the remaining streamlined cars were used as ARP shelters, one at Northfields and two at Cockfosters.

Production Trains

The large orders for new tube cars for the 1935–40 New Works Programme were based on the flat fronted design of the last six-car train of 1935 Experimental Tube Stock. The original idea of a 'high-speed tube train' was still very much alive, but without costly alteration to the power supply system, it was decided to dilute the proposed all-motor car formations with trailer cars – based on the six-doors-aside design (two double doors and end single doors) of the trailer cars built by BRCW and Gloucester in 1931, all vehicles having slightly tapered ends. To economise on the number of cabs required, intermediate motor cars without cabs would also be provided – the non-driving motor car (NDM) was thus born.

The 1938 Tube Stock was regarded as a design classic, which was enhanced until the early-1950s by the cream uprights between the windows. DM 11286 in ex-overhauled condition (April 1952) awaits departure from Edgware. *F.G. Reynolds*

Passing Berkhamsted on 8 June 1939, new cars of 1938 Tube Stock are on route for delivery to London Transport. The cars are (left to right) 11158, 10158 and 11157 and were part of a consignment of four motor cars which arrived on LT metals the same day. *H.C. Casserley*

The new 1938 cars were in many respects the same as units 10009–11009/10011–11011 of 1935 stock, but incorporating detail changes, often to tidy up the finished product by giving smoother and more rounded lines. End bays, for example, had four windows (the two centre ones with opening quarter lights and their adjacent ones as non-opening casements for the sliding doors) as with the centre bay. The five headlights were rounded instead of square and a three line box for destination plates was fitted above them, below the offside cab window. The interior ventilators over the communicating doors and over the door between the saloon and the cab were initially closely spaced vertically, but this was changed early on to be oval shaped. The initial trains also had smooth lines at the draught screen instead of being sharp-ended, but experience soon showed that passengers needed something to hold onto and thus hoop hand rails were fitted – and retro-fitted to those that were not originally provided. The tail lamp bracket, originally mounted on the front cab door was soon moved, offset under the driver's cab window towards the centre cab door. The train set number plates were located under the front cab door window, rather than at the bottom of the offside cab window. These differences made the 1938 Tube Stock what it was – a good looking train of modern appearance, its gentle curves and domed roof with wing-shaped ventilators giving a most acceptable finish.

The ordering of the 1938 Tube Stock is complex and figures changed no fewer than nine times between October 1935 and October 1938 before the ultimate totals (see table opposite) were arrived at. Whilst plans centred around new cars and the reallocation of existing ones for the 1935–40 New Works Programme extensions, some of the factors involved, over differing periods of time, included:

- Plans for a new depot at either Finchley Manor or Copthall Park on the extended routes proved impossible and a new depot was planned at Aldenham by extending the line north from the existing terminus at Edgware to Bushey Heath. Not being in previous plans, additional rolling stock would be required for this section.
- All Northern Line trains to be seven cars (instead of a mix of six and seven).
- Increase of Bakerloo Line trains from six to seven cars.
- Changing maintenance spares from 15% (motors) and 10% (trailers) to 12½% (for complete trains).
- The provision of 58 MCCW trailers of 1927 vintage to run with the new trains. These became available through stock reallocations and were modified to suit their new role. This included replacing the Ward mechanical couplers with semi-permanent bar couplings and the fitting of compressors.
- Increase in traffic levels on the Piccadilly Line between 1934 and 1938 as a result of the 1932–33 extensions, required additional cars.
- Operation of some nine-car trains on the Northern Line – ten such trains were ordered.

The number of new cars thus ordered totalled 1,121 to which must be added the experimental cars (24) and the 58 converted trailers of 1927 vintage. All driving motors were built by Metro Cammell and trailers by Birmingham. The NDMs were built by both companies.

1938	'A' DM	312		10012–10323
	'D' DM	312		11012–11323
	'A' DM (9 car)	10		90324–90333
	'D' DM (9 car)	10	644	91324–91333
	NDM (MCW)	57		12000–12028, 12409–12411, 12422–12446
	NDM (BRCW)	99		12059–12157
	NDM (MCW – 9 car)	50	206	92029–92058, 92447–92466
	Trailers	251		012158–012388, 012412–012421, 012467–012476
	Trailers (9 car)	20	271	092389–092408
	Total:		**1121**	
PLUS –				
1927	Trailers	58	58	70513–70570
1935	'A' DM (Streamlined)	9		10000–10008
	'D' DM (Streamlined)	9		11000–11008
	'A' DM (Flat front)	3		10009–10011
	'D' DM (Flat front)	3	24	11009–11011
	Total:		**1203**	

The first cars were delivered to Lillie Bridge on 11 May 1938 (driving motors 10012 and 11012), 24 May 1938 (NDM 12000) and 30 May 1938 (trailers 012158 – 012161) and were transported to Golders Green depot soon after. A Press Launch was held on 27 June 1938 and the first complete train entered service on 30 June on the Northern Line. The standard formation was seven cars, formed of a three- and four-car unit thus – M-T-NDM-M+M-T-M. By the end of November 1938, there were 24 trains available for service and with deliveries anticipated as continuing at two trains per week, attention turned additionally to the Bakerloo, to where the first train entered service on 2 January 1939 in the formation M-T-M+M-NDM-M. Soon it was decided to make all Bakerloo units M-T-M to reduce power consumption and more closely match the slower performance of the older trains, and nine such trains were running by the end of July 1939. Four-car trains also took over from the Pre-1938 Stock on the Metropolitan's Stanmore shuttle from 31 July 1939 and became part of the Bakerloo's allocation (less the NDMs) when the operation of the Stanmore line transferred to the Bakerloo on 20 November 1939.

With the decision to continue operating some nine-car trains on the Northern Line and the promise of such new trains at the end of the order, LT instead decided to put these into service as soon as possible in the latter part of 1938, requesting them to be delivered with urgency. Between February and May 1939 therefore, all 90 cars required for ten nine-car formations were delivered. Whilst identical in appearance, they were in fact, quite different in formation, requiring only two driving cabs per complete train. Because the driving motor cars and their adjacent NDM would have to stop in the tunnel at nominated locations, they did not have guard's panels. Instead these were provided on the NDMs at positions '3' and '7'. Emergency uncoupling was also provided between cars '2' and '3' and between '7' and '8', enabling at least seven cars to be shunted into a tunnel length siding, should it become defective. These couplers were 'Ward' mechanical couplers which were fitted upside down than usual (on Pre-1938 Tube Stock) to enable quick operation in emergency situations. Because the new nine-car trains were marginally longer than the nine-car trains of Pre-1938 Tube Stock, the outer end double doors were to remain closed until the relevant signalling modifications were carried out. Of the ten trains, two were to be spare – four were to operate between Edgware and Kennington and four between High Barnet and Kennington, but in the event only two ever operated on the former route, beginning on 19 June 1939. Prior to this, three seven-car trains of 'nine-car stock' began running on 15 May 1939 in nominated nine-car workings, with the other five by the end of June 1939. The formation of nine-car trains was thus: M-NDM+SNDM-T-NDM-T-SNDM+NDM-M.

A seven-car train of 1938 Tube Stock stands in platform No.3 at High Barnet, when new into service. Note the bracket for the tail lamp on the front cab door. These were soon relocated to under the driver's window. On the right, the stabling sidings for Underground trains are still under construction. *Charles F. Klapper/LURS*

Interior of 1938 Tube Stock when new and before the fitting of line diagrams and advertisements. Note the much smoother lines around the draught screens, although hoop grab rails were soon fitted. *LT Museum*

The beginning of the Second World War in September 1939 saw nine-car operation suspended and subsequently abandoned, although not officially so until 1946. Whilst its operation was successful, a number of points probably dealt its death blow:

- Only 25% of trips operated with nine-car trains were equivalent to an overcrowded seven-car train.
- The trains often caused minor irritations to services – more nine-car trains would possibly cause more significant delays.
- The areas of operation were restricted – one platform at Edgware, not south of Kennington and access to Golders Green depot only from the main running lines.

However, the nine-car stock trains continued running as seven-car block trains with both trailers removed and two NDM cars having the motors isolated. Moreover, the closure of the Strand–Kennington and London Bridge–Moorgate sections for tunnel strengthening (September to December 1939 and May 1940 respectively) resulted in seven-car formations being reduced to six, by the removal of the NDM car in four-car units. It was not always possible to restore the NDM to the original formation, despite the intention to do so.

It was decided that the LNER, on whose lines the extended Underground would operate, would have ownership of some cars, which included the Central and Northern lines. Probably for simplicity, the 1938 Tube Stock was chosen to represent both lines, although it would only operate on the Northern Line, and in any case was a 'paper' exercise, for London Transport still operated and maintained the cars. Nonetheless, special ownership plates 'Property of LNER' were attached to the sole bars of the 289 nominated cars, of which 129 were designated 'Central Line' and 160 'Northern Line' – none ever worked on the former!

'A' DMs	10238–10323	86
'D' DMs	11238–11323	86
NDMs	12117–12157	41
Trailers	012313–012388	76
Total:		**289**

All this became superfluous when, in 1948, LNER ownership ceased with the inauguration of the British Transport Commission, and the LTE took them over.

Enough new stock had been delivered to enable the Northern Line to be worked by all 1938 Tube Stock from 1942, along with 27 trains on the Bakerloo services. Although eight DMs, three NDMs, and 16 trailers were not delivered until after the cessation of hostilities, there were cars on London Transport metals that fell into the following categories:

- Delivered, commissioned, run in service and subsequently stored.
- Delivered, commissioned and subsequently stored.
- Delivered and stored.

The fact that the Bakerloo Line was operating a mix of old and new trains often caused severe disruptions especially at peak times, because of the lesser performance of the former. The situation improved slightly in early-1943 when five trains were transferred from the Northern Line and all but a handful of the Bakerloo's 1938 Tube Stock cars out of service with various defects were made good again. The following year, some of the stored cars around the network were made serviceable, increasing the line's 1938 stock by 8½ trains and making 49 available, with 42 in service. The balance of trains was made up by a handful of old Pre-1938 trains. This involved using 14 trailers from the nine-car scheme and modifying them for six-car operation. When converted they were renumbered from 09xxxx to A9xxxx. This was the preferred plan, rather than use the stored NDMs at Neasden and Stanmore, which were set aside for seven-car formations, which occurred in 1946/47.

The yearly statistics for the 1938 Tube Stock are shown below.

End year	As delivered					In service				
	M	NDM	T	Year total	Stock total	M	NDM	T	Year total	Stock total
1938	202	57	55	314	314	142	38	48	228	228
1939	270	106	132	508	822	296	97	108	501	729
1940	156	38	64	258	1080	137	45	65	247	976
1941	8	2	4	14	1094	19	8	12	39	1015
1942	–	–	–	–	1094	8	6	3	17	1032
1944	–	–	–	–	1094	34	–	13	47	1079
1946	6	3	7	16	1110	–	9	–	9	1088
1947	2	–	9	11	1121	5	–	4	9	1097
1948	–	–	–	–	1121	3	2	–	5	1102
1949	–	–	–	–	1121	–	1	14	15	1117
1951	–	–	–	–	1121	–	–	1	1	1118
1952	–	–	–	–	1121	–	–	3	3	1121
Total:	**644**	**206**	**271**	**1121**	**1121**	**644**	**206**	**271**	**1121**	**1121**

Short train operation in off-peak periods resumed on the Bakerloo Line in June 1950 and one such train is seen on the northbound at Dollis Hill. It comprises one of the trailers (second from front) of 1927 vintage that were converted to work with the 1938 stock, although most of these were formed into three-car units. *LT Museum*

Post-War Developments

It was not until the outstanding deliveries were made of the 27 cars that the Bakerloo Line could be rid, in May 1949, of the Pre-1938 Tube Stock, even though they were delivered in 1946–47 – priority was given to the Central Line extensions and rolling stock. The constant changes to formations, often through the abortive non-standard nine-car trains, meant the operation of 'block' seven-car trains, which occurred in several different formations over a period of time:

DM – NDM + SNDM – NDM – SNDM + NDM – DM
DM – T – NDM – SNDM + SNDM – T – DM
DM – NDM + SNDM – T – SNDM + NDM – DM
DM – NDM + SNDM – T – NDM – T – DM
DM – T – NDM – NDM – SNDM + NDM – DM

Meanwhile, plans were being drawn up for the final allocations of 1938 Tube Stock. However, some of the original plans had been abandoned, such as –

- Nine-car train operation.
- The deferment (and subsequent abandonment) of the remaining extensions to the Northern Line (Finsbury Park–Alexandra Palace, Mill Hill East–Edgware and Edgware–Bushey Heath).
- The operation of the three streamlined trains on the Piccadilly Line, each with a new trailer added.

The plans were many and varied, exactly as when the 1938 stock was being planned, with changes occurring frequently. Also influencing the plans was the desire to extend the Bakerloo Line south from Elephant and Castle to Camberwell which, along with improved services and a new depot at Stanmore, would require an additional 14 seven-car trains. 1938 Tube Stock was also proposed for the Northern City Line, which would enable the Pre-1938 Tube Stock there to go to the Piccadilly Line for improved services. For the latter, this included four-tracking from Acton Town to Hanger Lane Junction, a flyover at Rayners Lane and a new Piccadilly Line depot at Ickenham.

The country's economic crisis in the autumn of 1948 saw the Piccadilly Line improvement plans and the outstanding Northern Line extensions all abandoned. There was thus no need for the 1938 Tube Stock on the Northern City Line and rolling stock allocation plans were yet again revised. Although block trains were an accepted feature of operation, the mechanical couplers were useful but non-standard and required more staff to operate them as opposed to the automatic couplers. What was required was an automatic coupler in the middle of a seven-car train but without the expense of providing a fully operative cab. The Uncoupling Non-Driving Motor (UNDM) car concept was thus born – simplified driving controls were placed in a panel at the uncoupling end, the operator observing movement through the communicating door during shunting or emergency working conditions.

The final plan for the 1938 Tube Stock and its associated cars (of 1927/35 vintage) in 1938 was for 1,203 vehicles, made up of –

153 x 7-car trains	1071	
6 x 6-car trains	36	
10 x 9-car trains	90	
3 x 2-car trains	6	**1203**

Taking into account all the cars available, including the imbalance from abortive schemes, just 91 new cars would be required to make up a total of 184 x 7-car trains (115x7 Northern and 69x7 Bakerloo, inclusive of trains for the Camberwell extension) plus the 3x2 Central Line shuttles – 1,294 cars in all. The plans drawn up, however, included more than new stock. It also involved much conversion work, including:

- The 20 SNDMs converted to UNDMs.

- Two standard NDMs converted to UNDMs.

- Standardisation of other former nine-car stock (by removing guard's panels from SNDMs and fitting them on DMs), and replacing the Ward mechanical coupler with the semi-permanent bar type.

- The 18 streamlined motors converted to trailers. The three trailers (012412 – 012414) destined to lengthen these trains from six to seven-cars were originally planned to be delivered without compressors, because each train of 1935 stock already had three compressors, one on each 'A'-end car. These three cars were now absorbed into the 1938 stock fleet and were delivered with compressors – but not until after the war.

The new stock would number 70 UNDMs and 21 trailers, all of which were built by Birmingham. In almost all respects they appeared similar to their 1938 counterparts, but the main visible difference was that the communicating doors had a straight top to them, rather than a gentle curve. Technical differences included beamless shoegear and shoe lifting equipment on UNDM cars. They were all delivered with cream window pillars, LT side transfers, and passenger door controls fitted. Because of wartime conditions, the last four cars of 1938 Tube Stock did not enter service until after the first cars of 1949 Tube Stock had been delivered.

The first of the new UNDM cars arrived on 16 November 1951 but the first trailer was not delivered until 16 February 1952. The order was completed with the arrival of the last trailer on 15 November 1952 and the last UNDMs on 20 December 1952. The first UNDM entered service on 10 March 1952 and the first trailer on 10 October. All were in service by 21 January 1953 (UNDMs) and 21 July 1953 (trailers).

The economic crisis of 1949 had also caused the cancellation of the Bakerloo Line's Camberwell extension, a decision which was made in September 1950. By then the orders for the 1949 Tube Stock had been placed and the penalties in cancelling were probably almost as much as proceeding with it. To that end, it was decided to continue with the build but to re-allocate the stock – effectively there were 15 seven-car trains surplus, and it was decided that they should work on the Piccadilly Line. This enabled the transfer of some Pre-1938 Tube Stock trains from the Piccadilly Line to the Central, giving relief to a fleet, some of which was continuing to suffer from the six or seven years of open air storage, even though thoroughly rehabilitated. This enabled more eight-car trains to be formed and enabled some 53 cars in poor condition to be withdrawn.

Interior of 1949 Tube Stock UNDM 31042, looking towards the driving end and the closed shunting control panel to the left of the communicating door. This car spent much of its time on the Piccadilly Line. The 1938 and 1949 cars were almost indistinguishable in appearance, apart from the square-ended tops to the communicating doors. *LT Museum*

1949 Tube Stock UNDM 30044 is seen in Neasden depot when new, fitted with passenger open push-buttons and appropriate signage pointing to them, along with London Transport transfers on the car sides, a feature that was soon to disappear from all but driving motor cars. To the right of the communicating door can be seen a couple/uncouple switch, in the form of a barrel into which a key was inserted. *Harry Luff*

With a total of 92 UNDM cars (70 new and 22 conversions), there was an equal number of 'A' end and 'D' end cars, enabling 46 'block' trains to be formed, with opposite facing UNDMs ('A' and 'D') in the middle of seven-car trains. There were to be 27 such trains on the Northern, four on the Bakerloo and 15 on the Piccadilly. This meant that those on the Piccadilly Line would not uncouple to short trains and thus their use would be confined to peak hours only, while their older Pre-1938 stock counterparts would be working all day, every day. This was thought not to be a sensible option so it was decided that they should uncouple, causing yet another change of plan. In short, the 15 Piccadilly Line trains would be formed of conventional three- and four-car units, with the Bakerloo having 46 units with 'D' end UNDMs and the Northern Line 46 units with 'A' end UNDMs, these new cars no longer being required to couple in the middle of block trains. This resulted in the Northern Line having 69 seven-car trains conventionally formed, but highlighted another problem. If this line was to uncouple, it would need to use three-car units as well as four, but the former had only one compressor. All 69 three-car units therefore had a second compressor fitted and a letter 'C' added under the main 012xxx car number, enabling the Northern Line to run 'short' trains of both three- and four-car length in stock moves. It was usual for trains working via the City to be three cars and those via Charing Cross four cars.

Another problem came to light as a result of the Bakerloo Line having only eight conventionally formed trains, and 46 with middle UNDMs. When uncoupling at Watford, the uncoupled portion would have to be driven, UNDM leading, some two miles to Croxley Green depot. This was deemed to be unsuitable and the 15 Piccadilly Line M-T-M formations were effectively 'swapped' with the same number of M-T-UNDM units on the Bakerloo.

After extensive reforming, the final allocation of 184 seven-car trains was thus in 1953:

Piccadilly Line	15 x 7	M – T – UNDM + M – T – NDM – M
Bakerloo Line	31 x 7	M – T – UNDM + M – T – NDM – M
	23 x 7	M – T – M + M – T – NDM – M
Northern Line	46 x 7	M – T – NDM – M + UNDM – T – M
	69 x 7	M – T – NDM – M + M – T – M

The plan to form like numbered pairs of motor cars in each unit held good (e.g. 10012 at one end and 11012 at the other), but the utilisation of trailers and NDMs bore no relationship to the order of the driving motor cars. Indeed, whilst it was the intention that NDMs that were temporarily removed on the Northern Line to form six-car trains returned to their original units, the complexities of that line often resulted in them being formed back into any convenient unit.

The yearly statistics for the 1949 Tube Stock are shown below.

	As delivered				In service			
End year	UNDM	T	Year total	Stock total	UNDM	T	Year total	Stock total
1951	13	–	13	13	–	–	–	–
1952	57	21	78	91	67	13	80	80
1953	–	–	–	91	3	8	11	91
Total:	**70**	**21**	**91**	**91**	**70**	**21**	**91**	**91**

Post-War Conversions

Mention has been made briefly of the conversion work on the 1935/38 stock cars to fit in with post-war plans, some of which had overtaken pre-war plans.

The three flat-fronted two-car units of 1935 Tube Stock were brought out of store at Cockfosters depot and were taken to Acton Works for conversion to shuttle units for the eastern end of the Central Line, which was one of the unchanged plans, but was undertaken later than originally anticipated. Because they could be working alongside Pre-1938 Tube Stock on the main Central Line, the Wedgelock automatic couplers were replaced by mechanical 'Ward' couplers, with air hoses being added on the car ends. Passenger door control was fitted and compressors were fitted on every car. Guard's door controls were removed from the cabs and relocated at the trailing end of the 'D' cars only. Unlike their streamlined counterparts, the flat ended cars did not have an overhaul before being stored, so their bogies were replaced by those from the streamlined motor cars. The troublesome MV equipment was replaced by the PCM equipment from streamlined units 003, 007 and 008.

The converted units entered service on the Central Line shuttle (Loughton–Epping and, to a lesser extent, Hainault–Woodford) between October 1950 and January 1951, but returned to the Piccadilly Line in May 1954 to operate on the Holborn–Aldwych shuttle. On 3 April 1955 DM 11010 was damaged when it overran the stopping mark at Aldwych – its subsequent rebuilding saw it look more like 1938 stock, by having conventional side cab doors (that did not extend up into the curve of the roof) and its train set number in the (1938 stock replacement) front cab door instead of the offside driving cab window.

The two-car units of 1935 stock continued to work on the Holborn–Aldwych shuttle service until 1957. With the electrification of the Central Line's Epping–Ongar branch, two of these units (10009–11009 and 10010–11010) were transferred back to the Central Line on 6 July 1957 and 20 August 1957 respectively with passenger door control being reinstated. The third unit (10011–11011) was retained as a test train, being equipped for trials with regenerative braking equipment supplied by BTH in early 1957. Such tests began in May 1957 on the South Ealing test tracks. Later, GEC equipment was tested, followed by a Metropolitan Vickers system.

Meanwhile, the electrification of the Epping–Ongar branch from 18 November 1957 required two trains in service. A third (spare) was provided by borrowing a three-car unit of 1938 Tube Stock from the Northern Line (10177–012265–11177), being transferred on 16 November. Here it operated alongside the 1935 units. It was considered necessary to increase train lengths on the shuttle units and to that end, each received a suitably converted trailer of 1927 vintage during 1958, being provided with passenger door control. That for the test unit was stored until the tests were concluded (in 1960).

Work then began early in 1950 of the conversion of the 18 streamlined motor cars into trailers. The streamlined cab end had to be removed and then rebuilt into a conventional trailing end with single sliding doors. In common with other trailers, a compressor was fitted and the car rewired to trailer car requirements. Passenger door control was also fitted. The first to be completed was 012484 (ex-10007) in August 1950 and entered service on the Northern Line the next month. The completion of the other 17 cars was put on hold until operational experience had been gained with the first converted car. Only minor changes were necessary to door equipment and bogies and the others were completed between February 1951 and October 1952. The converted cars were 'similar' to their 1938 Stock counterparts, but retained the three windows (instead of four) in the end bays, their interior wing shaped ventilators over the communicating doors, and, on the original trailing end, slightly recessed communicating doors and windows. For a temporary period, until all the conversions under the 1949 programme were completed (in 1953), they worked in 'block' formations.

The next part of the programme was to convert the 20 SNDM cars to UNDMs, along with two ordinary NDMs, making 22 in all. On all cars, provision was made for shunting control equipment to be fitted in a cabinet at one end and, on the 20 SNDM cars, the guard's control panels were removed. At the shunting end, Wedgelock automatic couplers were fitted. The first converted car was 30015 (ex 92461), completed in December 1951. It entered service in February 1952 in block train formation with opposite facing UNDMs in the middle, comprising also a 1935 converted trailer. However, late deliveries of equipment meant that the UNDMs ran without shunt control equipment for a short period of time.

A three-car unit of 1938 Tube Stock was loaned to the Central Line from the end of 1957 to deputise for a unit of 1935 stock that was being used for engineering tests. It is seen at North Weald on 19 July 1957. *Alan A. Jackson*

The other work included converting the other nine-car NDMs to 'standard' NDMs and renumbering them from 92xxx to 12xxx. The NDMs which coupled to SNDMs by means of a 'Ward' coupler were converted to the normal semi-permanent bar coupling between intermediate cars. The DMs from nine-car trains were equipped with guard's controls and were renumbered from 90/91xxx to 10/11xxx.

When all the conversions were complete by the end of 1953, and after extensive reformation of units, the 1935 converted trailers ended up in three-car UNDM units on the Northern Line, while the new 1949 Stock trailers were formed up into Northern Line four-car units. The 58 'converted' trailers of 1927 vintage remained on the Bakerloo Line, with most (but not all) being in three-car units. The fleet was made up as follows:

1938	'A' DM	322		10012–10333
	'D' DM	322	644	11012–11333
	NDM (MCW)	85		12000–12054, 12056–12057, 12409–12411,
				12422–12446
	NDM (BRCW)	99	184	12059–12157
	Trailer	271	271	012158–012408, 012412–012421,
				012467–012476
	'A' UNDM	22	22	30000–30021
	Total:		**1121**	
PLUS –				
1927	Trailers	58	58	70513–70570
1935	'A' DM (Flat front)	3		10009–10011
	'D' DM (Flat front)	3		11009–11011
	Trailers	18	24	012477–012494
1949	'A' UNDM	24		30022–30045
	'D' UNDM	46		31000–31045
	Trailers	21	91	012495–012515
	Total:		**1294**	

The fleet total was increased by three to 1,297 in 1958, following the conversion of three Pre-1938 trailers (which became 70510–70512) to work with the 1935 stock motor cars on the Central Line shuttle services.

Driving motor car 10306 was modified in 1949 with windows extending up into the curve of the roof line, an idea proposed for the 1952 Tube Stock which was not, in the event, built. It is seen at the rear of a train departing Edgware. *Major E.A.S. Cotton*

Modifications

With any new rolling stock, early in-service experience often results in modifications being made. These are done to the existing trains and to those still outstanding to be completed. This was never more so than on the 1938 Tube Stock, where modifications were many and frequent, mainly because they were so revolutionary for their time. Never before had traction equipment and compressors to fit in a small area under the car floor. This apart, the 1938 Tube Stock also received modifications to determine improvements for future rolling stock, either in style, cars, a unit, a train, or a group of car types. Some of these are listed below:

- Although passenger door control was abandoned during the Second World War, it was necessary to make modifications, tried on a Northern Line train in 1940. These concepts were adopted but it was not until December 1949 (Bakerloo Line) and April 1950 (Northern Line) that it was reintroduced. Whilst the Piccadilly Line cars of 1938/49 Stock retained passenger door control, it was never used on that line and the relevant circuits and controls were isolated.

- A fore/aft traction brake controller on a DM car 10230 in 1951.

- Cars were originally delivered with the advertisements immediately above the cant rail and the line diagram above them. The positions were later reversed.

- During the Second World War, a trial was undertaken with positioning the car line diagram in a 'V' shape along the centre of the ceiling. It is thought that this modification was made on a stored car and not used in service.

- Ceiling fans were fitted to DM 10320 in 1947. This was developed so that a complete train was fitted in 1949, being 10138 and 012168 (by GEC), 12117 and 11138 (by the Patent Lighting Co.) and 10023, 012173 and 11023 (by J. Stone and Co.). The seven-car train also had outside door indicator lights fitted on the curve of the roof. This was initially a light in a flush fitting, but was later changed to be a raised glass dome to improve sighting by platform staff.

- A 'desk' type master controller was fitted in 1948 to DM 10230 prior to the delivery of the District Line 'R' Stock. A trial for the same new stock involved a fluid speedometer on DM 10210 in 1950.

- Fluorescent lights were fitted to DM 11294 in 1953, prior to the 1956 Tube Stock.

- DM 10306 was fitted in 1949 with taller windows. This was done in preparation for the planned but unrealised 1952 Tube Stock. The conversion on DM 10306 was done after a trial on a section of DM 11237, which was in Acton Works for repair, in the spring of 1949.

Cars converted and renumbered are shown after the initial list but such cars are identified * thus in the following lists.

1935 EXPERIMENTAL TUBE STOCK DRIVING MOTOR CARS

BUILT BY METROPOLITAN-CAMMELL – Total 24

'A'-END MOTOR CARS   'D'-END MOTOR CARS

Delivered	Entered service	Line	No.	Delivered	Entered service	Line	No.
02.10.36	08.04.37	P	10000*	02.10.36	08.04.37	P	11000*
23.10.36	05.08.37	P	10001*	23.10.36	05.08.37	P	11001*
05.11.36	08.04.37	P	10002*	05.11.36	08.04.37	P	11002*
05.03.37	15.04.37	P	10003*	05.03.37	15.04.37	P	11003*
21.05.37	28.06.37	P	10004*	21.05.37	28.06.37	P	11004*
28.04.37	03.08.37	P	10005*	28.04.37	03.08.37	P	11005*
30.03.37	01.06.37	P	10006*	30.03.37	01.06.37	P	11006*
08.05.37	10.06.37	P	10007*	08.05.37	10.06.37	P	11007*
25.06.37	19.07.37	P	10008*	25.06.37	19.07.37	P	11008*
07.08.37	24.01.38	P	10009	07.08.37	24.01.38	P	11009
02.09.37	10.03.38	P	10010	02.09.37	10.03.38	P	11010
22.10.37	24.01.38	P	10011	22.10.37	24.01.38	P	11011

1938 TUBE STOCK DRIVING MOTOR CARS

BUILT BY METROPOLITAN-CAMMELL – Total 624

'A'-END MOTOR CARS

Delivered	Entered service	Line	No.	Delivered	Entered service	Line	No.	Delivered	Entered service	Line	No.
11.05.38	30.06.38	N	10012	02.08.38	17.10.38	N	10039	03.10.38	24.10.38	N	10066
24.05.38	30.06.38	N	10013	13.08.38	13.09.38	N	10040	06.10.38	31.01.39	N	10067
24.05.38	06.07.38	N	10014	13.08.38	10.09.38	N	10041	14.10.38	14.11.38	N	10068
30.05.38	06.07.38	N	10015	22.08.38	12.10.38	N	10042	10.10.38	05.11.38	N	10069
21.06.38	27.07.44	B	10016	25.08.38	12.10.38	N	10043	10.10.38	17.12.38	N	10070
09.06.38	27.07.38	N	10017	25.08.28	02.01.39	B	10044	14.10.38	19.12.38	N	10071
14.06.38	27.07.38	N	10018	22.08.38	30.09.38	N	10045	22.10.38	28.12.38	N	10072
09.06.38	15.02.39	N	10019	29.08.38	04.10.38	N	10046	17.10.38	25.11.38	N	10073
21.06.38	04.08.38	N	10020	01.09.38	17.09.38	N	10047	22.10.38	25.11.38	N	10074
21.06.38	04.08.38	N	10021	01.09.38	31.10.38	N	10048	27.10.38	10.11.38	N	10075
01.07.38	19.11.39	N	10022	29.08.38	30.09.38	N	10049	24.10.38	01.12.38	N	10076
01.07.38	29.08.38	N	10023	08.09.38	05.11.38	N	10050	24.10.38	01.12.38	N	10077
27.06.38	06.03.40	N	10024	05.09.38	03.11.38	N	10051	27.10.38	10.11.38	N	10078
07.07.38	28.08.38	N	10025	05.09.38	27.10.38	N	10052	03.11.38	21.11.38	N	10079
07.07.38	28.08.38	N	10026	08.09.38	24.09.38	N	10053	31.10.38	28.11.38	N	10080
14.07.38	10.09.38	N	10027	12.09.38	02.01.39	N	10054	31.10.38	28.12.38	N	10081
04.07.38	23.09.38	N	10028	15.09.38	04.10.38	N	10055	03.11.38	17.11.38	N	10082
14.07.38	06.09.38	N	10029	12.09.38	24.09.38	N	10056	10.11.38	28.11.38	N	10083
25.07.38	13.09.38	N	10030	19.09.38	17.11.38	N	10057	07.11.38	25.11.38	N	10084
25.07.38	17.09.38	N	10031	15.09.38	14.11.38	N	10058	07.11.38	21.11.38	N	10085
19.07.38	06.09.38	N	10032	26.09.38	02.01.39	N	10059	10.11.38	25.11.38	N	10086
02.08.38	29.08.38	N	10033	19.09.38	12.12.38	N	10060	17.11.38	12.01.39	N	10087
02.08.38	03.09.38	N	10034	30.09.38	24.10.38	N	10061	14.11.38	14.01.39	N	10088
19.07.38	03.09.38	N	10035	26.09.38	17.10.38	N	10062	14.11.38	30.11.38	N	10089
25.07.38	12.10.38	N	10036	26.09.38	27.10.38	N	10063	17.11.38	02.01.39	N	10090
18.08.38	23.09.38	N	10037	30.09.38	31.10.38	N	10064	24.11.38	21.02.39	N	10091
18.08.38	12.10.38	N	10038	06.10.38	04.11.38	N	10065	22.11.38	05.12.38	N	10092

22.11.38	12.01.39	N	**10093**	15.05.39	30.05.39	N	**10153**	24.10.39	16.11.39	N	**10213**
24.11.38	02.01.39	B	**10094**	23.05.39	12.06.39	N	**10154**	30.10.39	28.11.39	N	**10214**
29.11.38	12.12.38	N	**10095**	31.05.39	22.06.39	N	**10155**	30.10.39	27.11.39	N	**10215**
29.11.38	23.01.39	N	**10096**	26.05.39	12.06.39	N	**10156**	30.10.39	28.11.39	N	**10216**
01.12.38	26.01.39	N	**10097**	08.06.39	28.06.39	N	**10157**	07.11.39	01.12.39	N	**10217**
01.12.38	19.12.38	N	**10098**	08.06.39	06.07.39	N	**10158**	07.11.39	01.12.39	N	**10218**
05.12.38	03.02.39	N	**10099**	16.06.39	01.07.39	N	**10159**	07.11.39	27.11.39	N	**10219**
12.12.38	16.01.39	B	**10100**	16.06.39	28.06.39	N	**10160**	13.11.39	09.12.39	N	**10220**
08.12.38	28.02.39	N	**10101**	19.06.39	01.07.39	N	**10161**	13.11.39	09.12.39	N	**10221**
08.12.38	16.01.39	N	**10102**	27.06.39	21.07.39	N	**10162**	22.11.39	18.12.39	N	**10222**
12.12.38	13.01.39	N	**10103**	22.06.39	15.07.39	N	**10163**	29.11.39	04.01.40	N	**10223**
12.12.38	16.01.39	B	**10104**	22.06.39	13.07.39	N	**10164**	22.11.39	09.12.39	N	**10224**
16.12.38	30.01.39	N	**10105**	04.07.39	25.07.39	N	**10165**	29.11.39	11.01.40	N	**10225**
16.12.38	03.02.39	N	**10106**	29.06.39	13.07.39	N	**10166**	29.11.39	04.01.40	N	**10226**
20.12.38	06.02.39	N	**10107**	29.06.39	18.07.39	N	**10167**	05.12.39	19.01.40	N	**10227**
20.12.38	03.02.39	B	**10108**	11.07.39	28.07.39	N	**10168**	05.12.39	24.01.40	N	**10228**
29.12.38	23.01.39	N	**10109**	07.07.39	21.07.39	N	**10169**	05.12.39	19.01.40	N	**10229**
29.12.38	23.01.39	N	**10110**	07.07.39	21.07.39	N	**10170**	12.12.39	24.02.40	N	**10230**
29.12.38	15.02.39	B	**10111**	18.07.39	31.07.39	N	**10171**	12.12.39	11.01.40	N	**10231**
29.12.38	03.02.39	B	**10112**	13.07.39	31.07.39	N	**10172**	12.12.39	24.01.40	N	**10232**
05.01.39	15.02.39	B	**10113**	13.07.39	27.07.39	N	**10173**	18.12.39	03.02.40	N	**10233**
05.01.39	02.03.39	N	**10114**	25.07.39	13.08.39	N	**10174**	18.12.39	02.02.40	N	**10234**
10.01.39	21.01.39	N	**10115**	22.07.39	04.08.39	N	**10175**	27.12.39	02.04.40	N	**10235**
10.01.39	23.01.39	N	**10116**	22.07.39	04.08.39	N	**10176**	27.12.39	30.03.40	N	**10236**
12.01.39	19.03.39	N	**10117**	25.07.39	21.08.39	N	**10177**	27.12.39	27.01.40	N	**10237**
12.01.39	06.02.39	N	**10118**	28.07.39	21.08.39	N	**10178**	09.01.40	13.04.40	N	**10238**
17.01.39	23.03.39	N	**10119**	28.07.39	21.08.39	N	**10179**	09.01.40	06.04.40	N	**10239**
17.01.39	28.02.39	N	**10120**	31.07.39	26.08.39	N	**10180**	09.01.40	12.02.40	N	**10240**
19.01.39	01.04.39	N	**10121**	04.08.39	24.08.39	N	**10181**	15.01.40	06.02.40	N	**10241**
19.01.39	19.03.39	N	**10122**	04.08.39	21.08.39	N	**10182**	15.01.40	21.02.40	N	**10242**
23.01.39	14.04.39	N	**10123**	09.08.39	26.08.39	N	**10183**	23.01.40	16.03.40	N	**10243**
23.01.39	23.03.39	N	**10124**	19.08.39	01.09.39	N	**10184**	23.01.40	23.02.40	N	**10244**
27.01.39	18.02.39	N	**10125**	19.08.39	29.08.39	N	**10185**	23.01.40	16.02.40	N	**10245**
27.01.39	18.02.39	N	**10126**	22.08.39	06.09.39	N	**10186**	08.02.40	01.03.40	N	**10246**
31.01.39	05.05.39	N	**10127**	25.08.39	11.09.39	N	**10187**	08.02.40	04.03.40	N	**10247**
31.01.39	01.04.39	N	**10128**	25.08.39	11.09.39	N	**10188**	08.02.40	08.03.40	N	**10248**
02.02.39	24.02.39	N	**10129**	29.08.39	16.09.39	N	**10189**	13.02.40	10.03.40	N	**10249**
02.02.39	24.02.39	N	**10130**	01.09.39	22.09.39	N	**10190**	13.02.40	16.05.40	N	**10250**
06.02.39	24.02.39	N	**10131**	01.09.39	16.09.39	N	**10191**	13.02.40	14.03.40	N	**10251**
06.02.39	18.02.39	N	**10132**	04.09.39	22.09.39	N	**10192**	19.02.40	18.05.40	N	**10252**
09.02.39	03.03.39	N	**10133**	12.09.39	29.09.39	N	**10193**	19.02.40	28.03.40	N	**10253**
13.02.39	03.03.39	N	**10134**	12.09.39	28.09.39	N	**10194**	19.02.40	01.05.40	N	**10254**
13.02.39	04.03.39	N	**10135**	12.09.39	07.10.39	N	**10195**	26.02.40	31.05.40	N	**10255**
13.02.39	04.03.39	N	**10136**	18.09.39	07.10.39	N	**10196**	26.02.40	02.05.40	N	**10256**
16.02.39	10.03.39	N	**10137**	18.09.39	13.10.39	N	**10197**	26.02.40	12.04.40	N	**10257**
16.02.39	09.03.39	N	**10138**	18.09.39	10.11.39	N	**10198**	04.03.40	09.10.40	N	**10258**
20.02.39	15.03.39	N	**10139**	25.09.39	16.10.39	N	**10199**	04.03.40	09.10.40	N	**10259**
23.02.39	15.03.39	N	**10140**	25.09.39	19.10.39	N	**10200**	04.03.40	11.05.40	N	**10260**
23.02.39	11.03.39	N	**10141**	25.09.39	13.10.39	N	**10201**	11.03.40	13.08.40	N	**10261**
27.02.39	05.05.39	N	**10142**	03.10.39	04.11.39	N	**10202**	11.03.40	20.08.40	B	**10262**
02.03.39	27.03.39	N	**10143**	03.10.39	25.10.39	N	**10203**	11.03.40	01.06.42	N	**10263**
06.03.39	31.03.39	N	**10144**	03.10.39	25.10.39	N	**10204**	18.03.40	25.04.40	N	**10264**
09.03.39	27.03.39	N	**10145**	10.10.39	04.11.39	N	**10205**	18.03.40	19.06.40	N	**10265**
16.03.39	31.03.39	N	**10146**	10.10.39	10.11.39	N	**10206**	18.03.40	06.05.40	N	**10266**
23.03.39	11.04.39	N	**10147**	10.10.39	10.11.39	N	**10207**	15.04.40	28.06.40	N	**10267**
30.03.39	11.04.39	N	**10148**	18.10.39	18.12.39	N	**10208**	15.04.40	29.05.40	N	**10268**
06.04.39	25.04.39	N	**10149**	18.10.39	09.12.39	N	**10209**	01.04.40	17.12.40	N	**10269**
21.04.39	01.06.39	N	**10150**	18.10.39	10.11.39	N	**10210**	22.04.40	17.06.40	N	**10270**
28.04.39	15.05.39	N	**10151**	24.10.39	16.11.39	N	**10211**	30.04.40	25.09.40	N	**10271**
09.05.39	22.05.39	N	**10152**	24.10.39	19.11.39	N	**10212**	15.04.50	09.05.40	N	**10272**

22.04.40	08.06.40	N	10273	10.06.40	06.11.40	N	10290	05.08.40	21.03.44	B	10307
30.04.40	18.05.40	N	10274	17.06.40	18.10.40	N	10291	26.08.40	09.04.44	B	10308
30.04.40	09.04.41	N	10275	17.06.40	18.10.40	N	10292	26.08.40	09.04.44	B	10309
07.05.40	25.09.40	N	10276	24.06.40	23.12.40	N	10293	02.09.40	21.03.44	B	10310
07.05.40	20.08.40	B	10277	24.06.40	02.01.41	N	10294	02.10.40	05.04.44	B	10311
07.05.40	06.06.40	N	10278	24.06.40	06.11.40	N	10295	17.12.40	10.03.44	B	10312
14.05.40	05.12.40	N	10279	01.07.40	27.06.41	N	10296	02.10.40	03.44	B	10313
14.05.40	05.12.40	N	10280	01.07.40	21.02.42	N	10297	02.10.40	05.04.44	B	10314
14.05.40	15.09.40	N	10281	15.07.40	22.05.41	N	10298	28.01.41	14.06.44	B	10315
28.05.40	24.06.40	N	10282	15.07.40	16.04.41	N	10299	17.12.40	23.02.44	B	10316
20.05.40	14.01.41	N	10283	15.07.40	28.04.41	N	10300	28.01.41	14.06.44	B	10317
28.05.40	21.04.42	N	10284	01.07.40	10.05.44	B	10301	25.02.41	15.03.44	B	10318
03.06.40	12.08.40	B	10285	29.07.40	21.03.41	N	10302	10.06.41	23.02.44	B	10319
28.05.40	13.08.40	B	10286	05.08.40	27.07.41	N	10303	03.05.46	19.07.47	B	10320
10.06.40	13.07.40	N	10287	19.07.40	18.03.42	N	10304	25.06.46	21.02.47	B	10321
03.06.40	12.08.40	B	10288	29.07.40	10.05.44	B	10305	15.01.47	05.03.48	B	10322
10.06.40	03.12.40	N	10289	02.09.40	15.03.44	B	10306	24.12.46	11.11.47	B	10323

'D'-END MOTOR CARS

Delivered	Entered service	Line	No.	Delivered	Entered service	Line	No.	Delivered	Entered service	Line	No.
11.05.38	30.06.38	N	11012	05.09.38	05.11.38	N	11050	14.11.38	14.01.39	N	11088
24.05.38	30.06.38	N	11013	08.09.39	03.11.38	N	11051	14.11.38	30.11.38	N	11089
24.05.38	06.07.38	N	11014	05.09.38	27.10.38	N	11052	17.11.38	02.01.39	N	11090
09.06.38	26.05.44	N	11015	12.09.38	24.09.38	N	11053	24.11.38	21.02.39	N	11091
14.06.38	06.07.38	N	11016	08.09.38	02.01.39	N	11054	22.11.38	05.12.38	N	11092
14.06.38	27.07.38	N	11017	15.09.38	04.10.38	N	11055	22.11.38	02.01.39	N	11093
09.06.38	27.07.38	N	11018	12.09.38	24.09.38	N	11056	24.11.38	02.01.39	B	11094
09.06.38	15.02.39	N	11019	15.09.38	17.11.38	N	11057	29.11.38	23.01.39	N	11095
21.06.38	04.08.38	N	11020	19.09.38	14.11.38	N	11058	29.11.38	12.12.38	N	11096
21.06.38	04.08.38	N	11021	19.09.38	02.01.39	N	11059	01.12.38	26.01.39	N	11097
27.06.38	19.11.39	N	11022	26.09.38	12.12.38	N	11060	01.12.38	19.12.38	N	11098
01.07.38	29.08.38	N	11023	30.09.38	24.10.38	N	11061	05.12.38	03.02.39	N	11099
27.06.38	06.03.40	N	11024	26.09.38	17.10.38	N	11062	12.12.38	16.01.39	B	11100
07.07.38	28.08.38	N	11025	30.09.38	27.10.38	N	11063	08.12.38	28.02.39	N	11101
07.07.38	28.08.38	N	11026	06.10.38	31.10.38	N	11064	08.12.38	16.01.39	N	11102
14.07.38	10.09.38	N	11027	03.10.38	04.11.38	N	11065	12.12.38	13.01.39	N	11103
04.07.38	23.09.38	N	11028	03.10.38	24.10.38	N	11066	12.12.38	16.01.39	B	11104
14.07.38	06.09.38	N	11029	06.10.38	31.01.39	N	11067	16.12.38	30.01.39	N	11105
25.07.38	13.09.38	N	11030	10.10.38	14.11.38	N	11068	16.12.38	03.02.39	N	11106
25.07.38	17.09.38	N	11031	14.10.38	05.11.38	N	11069	20.12.38	06.02.39	N	11107
02.08.38	06.09.38	N	11032	14.10.38	17.12.38	N	11070	20.12.38	03.02.39	B	11108
02.08.38	29.08.38	N	11033	17.10.38	25.11.38	N	11071	29.12.38	23.01.39	N	11109
19.07.38	03.09.38	N	11034	17.10.38	25.11.38	N	11072	29.12.38	23.01.39	N	11110
19.07.38	03.09.38	N	11035	22.10.38	28.12.38	N	11073	29.12.38	15.02.39	B	11111
18.08.38	12.10.38	N	11036	22.10.38	19.12.38	N	11074	29.12.38	03.02.39	B	11112
25.07.38	23.09.38	N	11037	27.10.38	10.11.38	N	11075	05.01.39	15.02.39	B	11113
02.08.38	12.10.38	N	11038	24.10.38	01.12.38	N	11076	05.01.39	02.03.39	N	11114
18.08.38	17.10.38	N	11039	24.10.38	01.12.38	N	11077	10.01.39	21.01.39	N	11115
13.08.38	13.09.38	N	11040	27.10.38	10.11.38	N	11078	10.01.39	23.01.39	N	11116
13.08.38	10.09.38	N	11041	03.11.38	21.11.38	N	11079	12.01.39	19.03.39	N	11117
25.08.38	12.10.38	N	11042	31.10.38	28.11.38	N	11080	12.01.39	06.02.39	N	11118
25.08.38	12.10.38	N	11043	31.10.38	28.11.38	N	11081	17.01.39	23.03.39	N	11119
22.08.38	02.01.39	B	11044	03.11.38	17.11.38	N	11082	17.01.39	28.02.39	N	11120
22.08.38	30.09.38	N	11045	10.11.38	28.11.38	N	11083	19.01.39	05.05.39	N	11121
01.09.38	04.10.38	N	11046	07.11.38	25.11.38	N	11084	19.01.39	19.03.39	N	11122
01.09.38	17.09.38	N	11047	07.11.38	21.11.38	N	11085	23.01.39	14.04.39	N	11123
29.08.38	31.10.38	N	11048	10.11.38	25.11.38	N	11086	23.01.39	23.03.39	N	11124
29.08.38	30.09.38	N	11049	17.11.38	12.01.39	N	11087	27.01.39	18.02.39	N	11125

27.01.39	18.02.39	N	**11126**	22.08.39	06.09.39	N	**11186**	08.02.40	01.03.40	N	**11246**
31.01.39	05.05.39	N	**11127**	25.08.39	11.09.39	N	**11187**	08.02.40	04.03.40	N	**11247**
31.01.39	01.04.39	N	**11128**	25.08.39	11.09.39	N	**11188**	08.02.40	08.03.40	N	**11248**
02.02.39	24.02.39	N	**11129**	29.08.39	16.09.39	N	**11189**	13.02.40	10.03.40	N	**11249**
02.02.39	24.02.39	N	**11130**	01.09.39	22.09.39	N	**11190**	13.02.40	16.05.40	N	**11250**
06.02.39	24.02.39	N	**11131**	01.09.39	16.09.39	N	**11191**	13.02.40	14.03.40	N	**11251**
06.02.39	18.02.39	N	**11132**	04.09.39	22.09.39	N	**11192**	19.02.40	18.05.40	N	**11252**
09.02.39	03.03.39	N	**11133**	12.09.39	29.09.39	N	**11193**	19.02.40	28.03.40	N	**11253**
13.02.39	03.03.39	N	**11134**	12.09.39	28.09.39	N	**11194**	19.02.40	01.05.40	N	**11254**
13.02.39	04.03.39	N	**11135**	12.09.39	07.10.39	N	**11195**	26.02.40	31.05.40	N	**11255**
13.02.39	04.03.39	N	**11136**	18.09.39	07.10.39	N	**11196**	26.02.40	02.05.40	N	**11256**
16.02.39	10.03.39	N	**11137**	18.09.39	13.10.39	N	**11197**	26.02.40	12.04.40	N	**11257**
16.02.39	09.03.39	N	**11138**	18.09.39	10.11.39	N	**11198**	04.03.40	09.10.40	N	**11258**
20.02.39	15.03.39	N	**11139**	25.09.39	16.10.39	N	**11199**	04.03.40	09.10.40	N	**11259**
23.02.39	15.03.39	N	**11140**	25.09.39	19.10.39	N	**11200**	04.03.40	11.05.40	N	**11260**
23.02.39	11.03.39	N	**11141**	25.09.39	13.10.39	N	**11201**	11.03.40	13.08.40	B	**11261**
27.02.39	05.05.39	N	**11142**	03.10.39	04.11.39	N	**11202**	11.03.40	20.08.40	B	**11262**
02.03.39	27.03.39	N	**11143**	03.10.39	25.10.39	N	**11203**	11.03.40	01.06.42	N	**11263**
06.03.39	31.03.39	N	**11144**	03.10.39	25.10.39	N	**11204**	18.03.40	25.04.40	N	**11264**
09.03.39	27.03.39	N	**11145**	10.10.39	04.11.39	N	**11205**	18.03.40	19.06.40	N	**11265**
16.03.39	31.03.39	N	**11146**	10.10.39	10.11.39	N	**11206**	18.03.40	06.05.40	N	**11266**
23.03.39	11.04.39	N	**11147**	10.10.39	10.11.39	N	**11207**	15.04.40	28.06.40	N	**11267**
30.03.39	11.04.39	N	**11148**	18.10.39	18.12.39	N	**11208**	15.04.40	29.05.40	N	**11268**
06.04.39	25.04.39	N	**11149**	18.10.39	09.12.39	N	**11209**	01.04.40	17.12.40	N	**11269**
21.04.39	01.06.39	N	**11150**	18.10.39	10.11.39	N	**11210**	22.04.40	17.06.40	N	**11270**
28.04.39	15.05.39	N	**11151**	24.10.39	16.11.39	N	**11211**	30.04.40	25.09.40	N	**11271**
09.05.39	22.05.39	N	**11152**	24.10.39	19.11.39	N	**11212**	15.04.50	09.05.40	N	**11272**
15.05.39	30.05.39	N	**11153**	24.10.39	16.11.39	N	**11213**	22.04.40	08.06.40	N	**11273**
23.05.39	12.06.39	N	**11154**	30.10.39	28.11.39	N	**11214**	30.04.40	18.05.40	N	**11274**
31.05.39	22.06.39	N	**11155**	30.10.39	27.11.39	N	**11215**	30.04.40	09.04.41	N	**11275**
26.05.39	12.06.39	N	**11156**	30.10.39	28.11.39	N	**11216**	07.05.40	25.09.40	N	**11276**
08.06.39	28.06.39	N	**11157**	07.11.39	01.12.39	N	**11217**	07.05.40	20.08.40	B	**11277**
08.06.39	06.07.39	N	**11158**	07.11.39	01.12.39	N	**11218**	07.05.40	06.06.40	N	**11278**
16.06.39	01.07.39	N	**11159**	07.11.39	27.11.39	N	**11219**	14.05.40	05.12.40	N	**11279**
16.06.39	28.06.39	N	**11160**	13.11.39	09.12.39	N	**11220**	14.05.40	05.12.40	N	**11280**
19.06.39	01.07.39	N	**11161**	13.11.39	09.12.39	N	**11221**	14.05.40	15.09.40	N	**11281**
27.06.39	21.07.39	N	**11162**	22.11.39	18.12.39	N	**11222**	28.05.40	24.06.40	N	**11282**
22.06.39	15.07.39	N	**11163**	29.11.39	04.01.40	N	**11223**	20.05.40	14.01.41	N	**11283**
22.06.39	13.07.39	N	**11164**	22.11.39	09.12.39	N	**11224**	28.05.40	21.04.42	N	**11284**
04.07.39	25.07.39	N	**11165**	29.11.39	11.01.40	N	**11225**	03.06.40	12.08.40	B	**11285**
29.06.39	13.07.39	N	**11166**	29.11.39	04.01.40	N	**11226**	28.05.40	13.08.40	B	**11286**
29.06.39	18.07.39	N	**11167**	05.12.39	19.01.40	N	**11227**	10.06.40	13.07.40	N	**11287**
11.07.39	28.07.39	N	**11168**	05.12.39	24.01.40	N	**11228**	03.06.40	12.08.40	B	**11288**
07.07.39	21.07.39	N	**11169**	05.12.39	19.01.40	N	**11229**	10.06.40	05.11.41	N	**11289**
07.07.39	21.07.39	N	**11170**	12.12.39	24.02.40	N	**11230**	10.06.40	06.11.40	N	**11290**
18.07.39	31.07.39	N	**11171**	12.12.39	11.01.40	N	**11231**	17.06.40	18.10.40	N	**11291**
13.07.39	31.07.39	N	**11172**	12.12.39	24.01.40	N	**11232**	17.06.40	18.10.40	N	**11292**
13.07.39	27.07.39	N	**11173**	18.12.39	03.02.40	N	**11233**	24.06.40	23.12.40	N	**11293**
25.07.39	13.08.39	N	**11174**	18.12.39	02.02.40	N	**11234**	24.06.40	02.01.41	N	**11294**
22.07.39	04.08.39	N	**11175**	27.12.39	02.04.40	N	**11235**	24.06.40	06.11.40	N	**11295**
22.07.39	04.08.39	N	**11176**	27.12.39	30.03.40	N	**11236**	01.07.40	27.06.41	N	**11296**
25.07.39	21.08.39	N	**11177**	27.12.39	27.01.40	N	**11237**	01.07.40	21.02.42	N	**11297**
28.07.39	21.08.39	N	**11178**	09.01.40	13.04.40	N	**11238**	15.07.40	22.05.41	N	**11298**
28.07.39	21.08.39	N	**11179**	09.01.40	06.04.40	N	**11239**	15.07.40	16.04.41	N	**11299**
31.07.39	26.08.39	N	**11180**	09.01.40	12.02.40	N	**11240**	15.07.40	28.04.41	N	**11300**
04.08.39	24.08.39	N	**11181**	15.01.40	06.02.40	N	**11241**	01.07.40	10.05.44	B	**11301**
04.08.39	21.08.39	N	**11182**	15.01.40	21.02.40	N	**11242**	29.07.40	21.03.41	N	**11302**
09.08.39	26.08.39	N	**11183**	23.01.40	16.03.40	N	**11243**	05.08.40	27.07.41	N	**11303**
19.08.39	01.09.39	N	**11184**	23.01.40	23.02.40	N	**11244**	19.07.40	18.03.42	N	**11304**
19.08.39	29.08.39	N	**11185**	23.01.40	16.02.40	N	**11245**	29.07.40	10.05.44	B	**11305**

02.09.40	15.03.44	B	**11306**	17.12.40	10.03.44	B	**11312**	25.02.41	15.03.44	B	**11318**
05.08.40	21.03.44	B	**11307**	02.10.40	08.03.44	B	**11313**	10.06.41	23.02.44	B	**11319**
26.08.40	09.04.44	B	**11308**	02.10.40	05.04.44	B	**11314**	03.05.46	19.07.47	B	**11320**
26.08.40	09.04.44	B	**11309**	28.01.41	14.06.44	B	**11315**	25.06.46	21.02.47	B	**11321**
02.09.40	21.03.44	B	**11310**	17.12.40	23.02.44	B	**11316**	15.01.47	05.03.48	B	**11322**
02.10.40	05.04.44	B	**11311**	28.01.41	14.06.44	B	**11317**	24.12.46	03.05.48	B	**11323**

1938 TUBE STOCK DRIVING MOTOR CARS FOR NINE-CAR TRAINS

BUILT BY METROPOLITAN-CAMMELL – Total 20

'A'-END MOTOR CARS

Delivered	Entered service	Line	No.	Delivered	Entered service	Line	No.	Delivered	Entered service	Line	No.
09.03.39	30.09.39	N	**90324***	13.04.39	15.05.39	N	**90328***	15.05.39	10.07.39	N	**90332***
16.03.39	19.06.39	N	**90325***	29.04.39	22.05.39	N	**90329***	22.05.39	01.07.39	N	**90333***
28.03.39	23.04.40	N	**90326***	01.05.39	19.06.39	N	**90330***				
03.04.39	19.06.39	N	**90327***	05.05.39	30.05.39	N	**90331***				

'D'-END MOTOR CARS

Delivered	Entered service	Line	No.	Delivered	Entered service	Line	No.	Delivered	Entered service	Line	No.
09.03.39	30.09.39	N	**91324***	13.04.39	15.05.39	N	**91328***	15.05.39	10.07.39	N	**91332***
16.03.39	19.06.39	N	**91325***	29.04.39	22.05.39	N	**91329***	22.05.39	01.07.39	N	**91333***
28.03.39	23.04.40	N	**91326***	01.05.39	19.06.39	N	**91330***				
03.04.39	19.06.39	N	**91327***	05.05.39	30.05.39	N	**91331***				

1938 TUBE STOCK NON-DRIVING MOTOR CARS

BUILT BY METROPOLITAN-CAMMELL – Total 57

Delivered	Entered service	Line	No.	Delivered	Entered service	Line	No.	Delivered	Entered service	Line	No.
24.05.38	20.06.38	N	**12000**	11.07.38	17.09.38	N	**12010**	25.07.39	21.08.39	N	**12020**
30.05.38	06.07.38	N	**12001**	11.07.38	10.09.38	N	**12011**	25.07.39	06.09.39	N	**12021**
09.06.38	15.02.39	N	**12002**	11.07.38	13.01.39	N	**12012**	31.07.39	26.08.39	N	**12022**
09.06.38	27.07.38	N	**12003**	31.05.39	28.06.39	N	**12013**	09.08.39	24.02.40	N	**12023**
21.06.38	04.08.38	N	**12004**	31.05.39	25.07.39	N	**12014**	22.08.39	01.03.40	N	**12024**
21.06.38	28.08.38	N	**12005**	19.06.39	01.07.39	N	**12015**	29.08.39	18.12.39	N	**12025**
27.06.38	06.03.40	N	**12006**	27.06.39	21.08.39	N	**12016**	04.09.39	18.12.39	N	**12026**
04.07.38	04.10.38	N	**12007**	04.07.39	04.08.39	N	**12017**	12.09.39	04.01.40	N	**12027**
04.07.38	23.09.38	N	**12008**	11.07.39	19.01.40	N	**12018**	18.09.39	17.01.40	N	**12028**
11.07.38	13.09.38	N	**12009**	18.07.39	31.07.39	N	**12019**				

Note that the remaining 28 cars are continued in the number series 12409–12411 and 12422–12446 below.

BUILT BY BIRMINGHAM – Total 99

Delivered	Entered service	Line	No.	Delivered	Entered service	Line	No.	Delivered	Entered service	Line	No.
18.07.38	12.10.38	N	12059	14.11.38	23.01.39	N	12092	08.09.39	24.01.40	N	12125
25.07.38	03.09.38	N	12060	21.11.38	02.01.39	N	12093	23.09.39	24.01.40	N	12126
25.07.38	29.08.38	N	12061	21.11.38	12.12.38	N	12094	11.10.39	09.01.40	N	12127
01.08.38	21.11.38	N	12062	28.11.38	21.02.39	N	12095	25.10.39	23.12.39	N	12128
01.08.38	17.11.38	N	12063	28.12.38	23.01.39	N	12096	08.11.39	17.02.40	N	12129
01.08.38	14.11.38	N	12064	05.12.38	30.01.39	N	12097	21.11.39	24.01.40	N	12130
15.08.38	06.09.38	N	12065	05.12.38	03.02.39	N	12098	18.12.39	12.02.40	N	12131
22.08.38	18.02.39	N	12066	12.12.38	06.02.39	N	12099	03.01.40	18.05.40	N	12132
22.08.38	05.12.38	N	12067	12.12.38	19.03.39	N	12100	15.01.40	24.01.40	N	12133
22.08.38	02.01.39	B	12068	19.12.38	11.04.39	N	12101	31.01.40	18.04.40	N	12134
29.08.38	17.12.38	N	12069	19.12.38	27.03.39	N	12102	15.02.40	30.03.40	N	12135
29.08.38	12.12.38	N	12070	02.01.39	03.03.39	N	12103	27.02.40	05.03.46	B	12136
29.08.38	30.09.38	N	12071	02.01.39	31.03.39	N	12104	11.03.40	25.04.40	N	12137
05.09.38	24.09.38	N	12072	09.01.39	09.03.39	N	12105	28.03.40	02.05.40	N	12138
12.09.38	03.11.38	N	12073	09.01.39	14.04.39	N	12106	22.04.40	16.05.40	N	12139
12.09.38	24.10.38	N	12074	16.01.39	15.03.39	N	12107	25.04.40	28.03.46	B	12140
12.09.38	31.10.38	N	12075	16.01.39	24.02.39	N	12108	29.04.40	10.06.40	N	12141
19.09.38	04.11.38	N	12076	24.01.39	05.05.39	N	12109	29.04.40	05.01.42	N	12142
19.09.38	27.10.38	N	12077	30.01.39	01.04.39	N	12110	05.05.40	29.05.40	N	12143
26.09.38	17.10.38	N	12078	06.02.39	04.03.39	N	12111	19.05.40	21.04.42	N	12144
26.09.38	12.10.38	N	12079	13.02.39	05.05.39	N	12112	19.05.40	24.06.40	N	12145
10.10.38	25.11.38	N	12080	20.02.39	13.07.39	N	12113	27.05.40	04.04.46	B	12146
10.10.38	30.11.38	N	12081	13.03.39	25.04.39	N	12114	02.06.40	24.01.42	N	12147
10.10.38	10.11.38	N	12082	27.03.39	23.02.40	N	12115	16.06.40	22.04.41	N	12148
24.10.38	12.01.39	N	12083	08.04.39	21.02.40	N	12116	04.11.40	10.12.46	B	12149
17.10.38	25.11.38	N	12084	01.05.39	22.05.39	N	12117	04.11.40	18.03.42	N	12150
24.10.38	01.12.38	N	12085	16.05.39	30.05.39	N	12118	14.11.40	27.06.41	N	12151
31.10.38	21.07.39	N	12086	27.05.39	12.06.39	N	12119	14.11.40	22.05.41	N	12152
31.10.38	15.07.39	N	12087	19.06.39	21.07.39	N	12120	28.04.41	26.11.41	N	12153
31.10.38	28.02.39	N	12088	03.07.39	23.12.39	N	12121	09.06.41	25.11.41	N	12154
08.11.38	28.11.38	N	12089	17.07.39	13.08.39	N	12122	20.11.46	03.05.48	B	12155
08.12.38	28.12.38	N	12090	31.07.39	01.09.39	N	12123	20.11.46	05.03.48	B	12156
14.11.38	19.12.38	N	12091	21.08.39	18.12.39	N	12124	12.12.46	18.03.49	B	12157

BUILT BY METROPOLITAN-CAMMELL – Continued from series 12000–12028

Delivered	Entered service	Line	No.	Delivered	Entered service	Line	No.	Delivered	Entered service	Line	No.
25.09.39	17.01.40	N	12409	05.12.39	13.05.46	B	12429	15.04.40	09.05.40	N	12439
03.10.39	06.01.40	N	12410	15.01.40	26.01.40	N	12430	22.04.40	17.06.40	N	12440
10.10.39	20.12.39	N	12411	08.02.40	08.03.40	N	12431	30.04.40	18.05.40	N	12441
18.10.39	21.12.39	N	12422	13.02.40	13.04.40	N	12432	07.05.40	06.06.40	N	12442
24.10.39	17.02.40	N	12423	19.02.40	01.05.40	N	12433	14.05.40	21.03.41	N	12443
30.10.39	02.02.40	N	12424	26.02.40	01.04.40	N	12434	20.05.40	23.05.41	N	12444
07.11.39	26.05.46	B	12425	04.03.40	11.05.40	N	12435	28.05.40	13.05.42	N	12445
13.11.39	30.12.39	N	12426	11.03.40	09.06.46	B	12436	03.06.40	05.05.42	N	12446
22.11.39	03.04.46	B	12427	18.03.40	06.05.40	N	12437				
29.11.39	03.05.46	B	12428	01.04.40	28.04.41	N	12438				

1938 TUBE STOCK NON-DRIVING MOTOR CARS FOR NINE-CAR TRAINS

BUILT BY METROPOLITAN-CAMMELL – Total 50

Delivered	Entered service	Line	No.	Delivered	Entered service	Line	No.	Delivered	Entered service	Line	No.
23.03.39	23.04.40	N	92029*	28.03.39	19.06.39	N	92046*	29.04.39	22.05.39	N	92451*
20.02.39	22.05.39	N	92030*	28.03.39	15.05.39	N	92047*	29.04.39	22.05.39	N	92452*
23.03.39	15.05.39	N	92031*	23.05.39	19.06.39	N	92048*	01.05.39	30.05.39	N	92453*
23.03.39	10.07.39	N	92032*	28.03.39	01.07.39	N	92049*	29.04.39	30.05.39	N	92454*
20.02.39	23.04.40	N	92033*	28.03.39	19.06.39	N	92050*	01.05.39	01.07.39	N	92455*
30.03.39	19.06.39	N	92034*	23.05.39	19.06.39	N	92051*	01.05.39	19.06.39	N	92456*
30.03.39	30.09.39	N	92035*	03.04.39	23.04.40	N	92052*	09.05.39	19.06.39	N	92457*
27.02.39	15.05.39	N	92036*	03.04.39	01.07.39	N	92053*	01.05.39	01.07.39	N	92458*
23.03.39	10.07.39	N	92037*	31.05.39	01.07.39	N	92054*	09.05.39	19.06.39	N	92459*
30.03.39	30.05.39	N	92038*	13.04.39	22.05.39	N	92055*	09.05.39	23.04.40	N	92460*
27.02.39	17.02.40	N	92039*	13.04.39	22.05.39	N	92056*	15.05.39	30.09.39	N	92461*
06.04.39	19.06.39	N	92040*	31.05.39	10.07.39	N	92057*	09.05.39	19.06.39	N	92462*
06.04.39	19.06.39	N	92041*	29.04.39	30.05.39	N	92058*	15.05.39	10.07.39	N	92463*
06.03.39	30.05.39	N	92042*	03.04.39	15.05.39	N	92447*	15.05.39	30.09.39	N	92464*
30.03.39	30.09.39	N	92043*	03.04.39	15.05.39	N	92448*	23.05.39	23.04.40	N	92465*
06.04.39	19.06.39	N	92044*	13.04.39	19.06.39	N	92449*	15.05.39	10.07.39	N	92466*
23.05.39	19.06.39	N	92045*	13.04.39	19.06.39	N	92450*				

1938 TUBE STOCK TRAILERS

BUILT BY BIRMINGHAM – Total 251

Delivered	Entered service	Line	No.	Delivered	Entered service	Line	No.	Delivered	Entered service	Line	No.
30.05.38	30.06.38	N	012158	29.08.38	04.10.38	N	012184	12.12.38	26.01.39	N	012210
30.05.38	30.06.38	N	012159	05.09.38	24.09.38	N	012185	19.12.38	03.02.39	N	012211
30.05.38	06.07.38	N	012160	05.09.38	24.09.38	N	012186	19.12.38	03.02.39	N	012212
30.05.38	06.07.38	N	012161	05.09.38	30.09.38	N	012187	02.01.39	02.03.39	N	012213
17.06.38	27.07.38	N	012162	12.09.38	24.10.38	N	012188	09.01.39	28.02.39	N	012214
17.06.38	27.07.38	N	012163	19.09.38	24.10.38	N	012189	09.01.39	28.02.39	N	012215
27.06.38	06.09.38	N	012164	19.09.38	12.10.38	N	012190	16.01.39	21.02.39	N	012216
27.06.38	10.09.38	N	012165	26.09.38	12.10.38	N	012191	24.01.39	23.03.39	N	012217
27.06.38	03.09.38	N	012166	26.09.38	02.01.39	B	012192	24.01.39	14.04.39	N	012218
27.06.38	10.09.38	N	012167	10.10.38	03.11.38	N	012193	24.01.39	23.03.39	N	012219
04.07.38	04.08.38	N	012168	10.10.38	31.10.38	N	012194	30.01.39	01.04.39	N	012220
04.07.38	04.08.38	N	012169	10.10.38	05.11.38	N	012195	30.01.39	05.05.39	N	012221
04.07.38	05.12.38	N	012170	10.10.38	31.10.38	N	012196	06.02.39	04.03.39	N	012222
04.07.38	05.12.38	N	012171	10.10.38	27.10.38	N	012197	06.02.39	10.03.39	N	012223
13.07.38	28.08.38	N	012172	17.10.38	25.11.38	N	012198	06.02.39	04.03.39	N	012224
13.07.38	29.08.38	N	012173	17.10.38	30.11.38	N	012199	13.02.39	15.03.39	N	012225
13.07.38	13.09.38	N	012174	24.10.38	01.12.38	N	012200	13.02.39	11.03.49	N	012226
13.07.38	17.09.38	N	012175	24.10.38	01.12.38	N	012201	20.02.39	05.05.39	N	012227
18.07.38	12.10.38	N	012176	08.11.38	28.12.38	N	012202	20.02.39	27.03.39	N	012228
18.07.38	13.09.38	N	012177	08.11.38	25.11.38	N	012203	20.02.39	15.03.39	N	012229
18.07.38	23.09.38	N	012178	14.11.38	28.12.38	N	012204	27.02.39	27.03.39	N	012230
25.07.38	28.08.38	N	012179	21.11.38	12.01.39	N	012205	06.03.39	31.03.39	N	012231
25.07.38	03.09.38	N	012180	21.11.38	12.01.39	N	012206	06.03.39	31.03.39	N	012232
01.08.38	05.12.38	N	012181	28.11.38	15.03.39	N	012207	20.03.39	11.04.39	N	012233
15.08.38	06.09.38	N	012182	05.12.38	19.12.38	N	012208	20.03.39	11.04.39	N	012234
22.08.38	30.09.38	N	012183	05.12.38	17.12.38	N	012209	03.04.39	01.06.39	N	012235

03.04.39	25.04.39 N	**012236**	02.10.39	25.10.39 N	**012294**	04.03.40	09.10.40 N	**012352**
25.04.39	22.05.39 N	**012237**	11.10.39	28.11.39 N	**012295**	04.03.40	09.10.40 N	**012353**
25.04.39	15.05.39 N	**012238**	11.10.39	10.11.39 N	**012296**	04.03.40	06.11.40 N	**012354**
08.05.39	24.02.40 N	**012239**	17.10.39	27.11.39 N	**012297**	11.03.40	25.04.40 N	**012355**
08.05.39	14.03.40 N	**012240**	17.10.39	19.11.39 N	**012298**	11.03.40	08.06.40 N	**012356**
16.05.39	12.06.39 N	**012241**	17.10.39	10.11.39 N	**012299**	11.03.40	19.06.40 N	**012357**
16.05.39	30.05.39 N	**012242**	17.10.39	28.11.39 N	**012300**	18.03.40	13.04.40 N	**012358**
22.05.39	28.06.39 N	**012243**	25.10.39	16.11.39 N	**012301**	18.03.40	21.03.41 N	**012359**
22.05.39	01.07.39 N	**012244**	25.10.39	16.11.39 N	**012302**	18.03.40	22.05.41 N	**012360**
22.05.39	28.06.39 N	**012245**	04.11.39	27.11.39 N	**012303**	28.03.40	02.05.40 N	**012361**
22.05.39	01.07.39 N	**012246**	04.11.39	01.12.39 N	**012304**	28.03.40	01.05.40 N	**012362**
27.05.39	22.06.39 N	**012247**	04.11.39	09.12.39 N	**012305**	28.03.40	18.05.40 N	**012363**
27.05.39	12.06.39 N	**012248**	04.11.39	01.12.39 N	**012306**	08.04.40	31.05.40 N	**012364**
13.06.39	06.07.39 N	**012249**	08.11.39	19.01.40 N	**012307**	08.04.40	06.06.40 N	**012365**
13.06.39	18.07.39 N	**012250**	08.11.39	11.01.40 N	**012308**	08.04.40	06.05.40 N	**012366**
13.06.39	13.07.39 N	**012251**	13.11.39	09.12.39 N	**012309**	22.04.40	16.05.40 N	**012367**
13.06.39	13.07.39 N	**012252**	13.11.39	18.12.39 N	**012310**	22.04.40	21.05.40 N	**012368**
19.06.39	21.07.39 N	**012253**	13.11.39	09.12.39 N	**012311**	22.04.40	20.05.40 N	**012369**
19.06.39	04.08.39 N	**012254**	13.11.39	09.12.39 N	**012312**	25.04.40	18.10.40 N	**012370**
27.06.39	15.07.39 N	**012255**	21.11.39	19.01.40 N	**012313**	25.04.40	18.10.40 N	**012371**
27.06.39	21.07.39 N	**012256**	21.11.39	11.01.40 N	**012314**	29.04.40	28.06.40 N	**012372**
27.06.39	21.07.39 N	**012257**	27.11.39	18.12.39 N	**012315**	29.04.40	12.08.40 B	**012373**
27.06.39	28.07.39 N	**012258**	27.11.39	04.01.40 N	**012316**	19.05.40	21.04.42 N	**012374**
03.07.39	31.07.39 N	**012259**	27.11.39	04.01.40 N	**012317**	05.05.40	29.05.40 N	**012375**
03.07.39	21.08.39 N	**012260**	18.12.39	12.02.40 N	**012318**	19.05.40	24.06.40 N	**012376**
10.07.39	31.07.39 N	**012261**	18.12.39	16.02.40 N	**012319**	27.05.40	01.06.42 N	**012377**
10.07.39	21.08.39 N	**012262**	18.12.39	10.03.40 N	**012320**	27.05.40	06.11.40 N	**012378**
10.07.39	04.08.39 N	**012263**	27.12.39	27.01.40 N	**012321**	02.06.40	13.08.40 B	**012379**
10.07.39	25.07.39 N	**012264**	27.12.39	24.01.40 N	**012322**	10.06.40	13.07.40 N	**012380**
17.07.39	21.08.39 N	**012265**	27.12.39	02.02.40 N	**012323**	10.06.40	12.08.40 B	**012381**
17.07.39	13.08.39 N	**012266**	27.12.39	24.01.40 N	**012324**	16.06.40	20.08.40 B	**012382**
24.07.39	29.08.39 N	**012267**	03.01.40	18.05.40 N	**012325**	01.07.40	13.08.40 B	**012383**
24.07.39	11.09.39 N	**012268**	03.01.40	11.05.40 N	**012326**	01.07.40	20.08.40 B	**012384**
24.07.39	26.08.39 N	**012269**	03.01.40	09.05.40 N	**012327**	04.11.40	23.12.40 N	**012385**
24.07.39	06.09.39 N	**012270**	08.01.40	04.03.40 N	**012328**	04.11.40	02.01.41 N	**012386**
31.07.39	21.08.39 N	**012271**	08.01.40	06.02.40 N	**012329**	14.11.40	14.01.41 N	**012387**
31.07.39	01.09.39 N	**012272**	08.01.40	03.02.40 N	**012330**	14.11.40	31.01.41 N	**012388**
05.08.39	11.09.39 N	**012273**	15.01.40	05.04.44 N	**012331**	11.04.47	20.11.47 B	**012412**
05.08.39	24.08.39 N	**012274**	15.01.40	09.04.44 B	**012332**	11.04.47	20.11.47 B	**012413**
05.08.39	21.08.39 N	**012275**	15.01.40	09.04.44 B	**012333**	15.07.47	12.04.49 B	**012414**
05.08.39	26.08.39 N	**012276**	23.01.40	02.04.40 N	**012334**	28.04.41	27.07.41 N	**012415**
21.08.39	22.09.39 N	**012277**	23.01.40	28.03.40 N	**012335**	28.04.41	27.06.41 N	**012416**
21.08.39	16.09.39 N	**012278**	23.01.40	16.03.40 N	**012336**	28.04.41	18.02.42 N	**012417**
28.08.39	16.09.39 N	**012279**	31.01.40	12.04.40 N	**012337**	09.06.41	05.11.41 N	**012418**
28.08.39	28.09.39 N	**012280**	31.01.40	30.03.40 N	**012338**	19.08.46	10.02.49 N	**012419**
28.08.39	22.09.39 N	**012281**	31.01.40	06.04.40 N	**012339**	19.08.46	11.02.49 N	**012420**
28.08.39	29.09.39 N	**012282**	13.02.40	17.06.40 N	**012340**	19.08.46	04.04.49 N	**012421**
08.09.39	16.10.39 N	**012283**	13.02.40	23.05.40 N	**012341**	19.08.46	01.05.52 N	**012467**
08.09.39	19.10.39 N	**012284**	13.02.40	22.05.40 N	**012342**	08.10.46	19.07.47 B	**012468**
15.09.39	04.11.39 N	**012285**	15.02.40	05.12.40 N	**012343**	08.10.46	21.02.47 B	**012469**
15.09.39	13.10.39 N	**012286**	15.02.40	17.12.40 N	**012344**	12.12.46	03.03.49 N	**012470**
15.09.39	13.10.39 N	**012287**	15.02.40	05.12.40 N	**012345**	15.01.47	20.04.49 N	**012471**
15.09.39	07.10.39 N	**012288**	23.02.40	05.04.41 N	**012346**	15.01.47	10.05.49 N	**012472**
23.09.39	07.10.39 N	**012289**	23.02.40	16.04.41 N	**012347**	27.03.47	24.11.51 B	**012473**
23.09.39	10.11.39 N	**012290**	23.02.40	28.04.41 N	**012348**	27.03.47	22.01.52 N	**012474**
02.10.39	10.11.39 N	**012291**	27.02.40	25.09.40 N	**012349**	15.07.47	06.05.49 B	**012475**
02.10.39	04.11.39 N	**012292**	27.02.40	09.04.41 N	**012350**	31.07.47	21.03.52 N	**012476**
02.10.39	25.10.39 N	**012293**	27.02.40	25.09.40 N	**012351**			

1938 TUBE STOCK TRAILERS FOR NINE-CAR TRAINS

BUILT BY BIRMINGHAM – Total 20

Delivered	Entered service	Line	No.	Delivered	Entered service	Line	No.	Delivered	Entered service	Line	No.
27.02.39	19.06.39	N	092389*	20.03.49	19.06.39	N	092396*	25.04.39	25.05.49	N	092403*
27.02.39	19.06.39	N	092390*	27.03.39	14.06.44	B	092397*	25.04.39	10.05.44	B	092404*
06.03.39	15.03.44	B	092391*	27.03.39	14.06.44	B	092398*	01.05.39	04.05.44	N	092405*
06.03.39	21.03.44	B	092392*	03.04.39	21.03.44	B	029399*	01.05.39	04.05.44	N	092406*
13.03.39	23.02.44	B	092393*	03.04.39	15.03.44	B	092400*	08.05.39	30.03.49	N	029407*
13.03.39	30.03.49	N	092394*	08.04.39	10.05.44	B	092401*	08.05.39	25.05.49	N	092408*
20.03.39	19.06.39	N	092395*	08.04.39	05.04.44	B	092402*				

1949 TUBE STOCK TRAILERS

BUILT BY BIRMINGHAM – Total 21

Delivered	Entered service	Line	No.	Delivered	Entered service	Line	No.	Delivered	Entered service	Line	No.
16.02.52	23.10.52	N	012495	19.04.52	21.07.53	N	012502	05.07.52	10.10.52	N	012509
23.02.52	15.10.52	N	012496	03.05.52	05.02.53	N	012503	12.07.52	20.11.52	N	012510
01.03.52	31.10.52	N	012497	10.05.52	07.11.52	N	012504	26.07.52	21.11.52	N	012511
08.03.52	30.10.52	N	012498	24.05.52	17.03.53	N	012505	16.08.52	05.05.53	N	012512
15.03.52	21.01.53	N	012499	07.06.52	12.06.53	N	012506	30.08.52	15.05.53	N	012513
27.03.52	02.01.53	N	012500	14.06.52	04.12.52	N	012507	27.10.52	05.12.52	N	012514
05.04.52	05.11.52	N	012501	21.06.52	22.10.52	N	012508	15.11.52	19.12.52	N	012515

1949 TUBE STOCK UNCOUPLING NON-DRIVING MOTOR CARS

BUILT BY BIRMINGHAM – Total 71

'A'-END UNDMs

Delivered	Entered service	Line	No.	Delivered	Entered service	Line	No.	Delivered	Entered service	Line	No.
07.12.51	14.03.52	N	30022	01.03.52	30.12.52	N	30030	24.05.52	24.06.52	N	30038
16.11.51	02.12.52	N	30023	15.03.52	21.04.52	N	30031	07.06.52	01.10.52	N	30039
24.11.51	04.12.52	N	30024	27.03.52	07.05.52	N	30032	14.06.52	22.10.52	N	30040
07.12.51	19.04.52	N	30025	27.03.52	12.05.52	N	30033	28.06.52	10.10.52	N	30041
07.12.51	12.11.52	N	30026	19.04.52	09.05.52	N	30034	05.07.52	31.10.52	N	30042
09.02.52	21.03.52	N	30027	26.04.52	28.05.52	N	30035	19.07.52	15.10.52	N	30043
16.02.52	21.03.52	N	30028	03.05.52	10.07.52	N	30036	26.07.52	24.09.52	B	30044
23.02.52	21.11.52	N	30029	19.05.52	19.12.52	N	30037	23.08.52	20.11.52	N	30045

'D'-END UNDMs

Delivered	Entered service	Line	No.	Delivered	Entered service	Line	No.	Delivered	Entered service	Line	No.
16.11.51	29.10.52	B	**31000**	27.01.52	01.10.52	N	**31016**	21.06.52	13.01.53	P	**31032**
24.11.51	23.10.52	B	**31001**	02.02.52	16.04.52	N	**31017**	28.06.52	03.11.52	P	**31033**
07.12.51	22.05.52	N	**31002**	02.02.52	10.10.52	B	**31018**	12.07.52	20.10.52	P	**31034**
07.12.51	28.05.52	B	**31003**	09.02.52	10.03.52	B	**31019**	19.07.52	02.09.52	N	**31035**
07.12.51	30.10.52	B	**31004**	16.02.52	03.04.52	N	**31020**	16.08.52	04.10.52	P	**31036**
15.12.51	09.05.52	N	**31005**	01.03.52	21.03.52	N	**31021**	23.08.52	15.10.52	P	**31037**
15.12.51	19.06.52	B	**31006**	08.03.52	31.03.52	B	**31022**	30.08.52	04.10.52	P	**31038**
29.12.51	14.03.52	N	**31007**	15.03.52	07.04.52	B	**31023**	06.09.52	15.10.52	N	**31039**
05.01.52	01.11.52	B	**31008**	27.03.52	12.05.52	N	**31024**	18.10.52	02.12.52	P	**31040**
05.01.52	03.10.52	B	**31009**	05.04.52	23.07.52	N	**31025**	18.10.52	18.11.52	P	**31041**
05.01.52	21.04.52	N	**31010**	19.04.52	03.06.52	B	**31026**	27.10.52	30.12.52	P	**31042**
12.01.52	14.10.52	B	**31011**	26.04.52	28.05.52	N	**31027**	15.11.52	20.12.52	N	**31043**
12.01.52	17.10.52	B	**31012**	10.05.52	10.07.52	N	**31028**	20.12.52	21.01.53	N	**31044**
12.01.52	17.10.52	B	**31013**	19.05.52	17.06.52	B	**31029**	20.12.52	14.01.53	N	**31045**
27.01.52	05.09.52	B	**31014**	07.06.52	15.08.52	N	**31030**				
19.01.52	23.09.52	N	**31015**	07.06.52	14.07.52	N	**31031**				

CARS CONVERTED AND RENUMBERED

CONVERSION OF 1935 TUBE STOCK 'STREAMLINED' MOTOR CARS TO TRAILERS:

Orig. No.	Reno.	Date	Orig. No	Reno.	Date	Orig. No.	Reno.	Date
10000	**012477**	07.05.51	10006	**012483**	19.02.51	11003	**012489**	08.01.51
10001	**012478**	25.05.51	10007	**012484**	31.08.50	11004	**012490**	02.03.51
10002	**012479**	20.07.51	10008	**012485**	30.11.50	11005	**012491**	03.11.50
10003	**012480**	18.01.51	11000	**012486**	20.04.51	11006	**012492**	30.03.51
10004	**012481**	09.02.51	11001	**012487**	20.06.51	11007	**012493**	26.09.50
10005	**012482**	12.10.50	11002	**012488**	23.09.51	11008	**012494**	15.12.50

CONVERSION OF NINE-CAR STOCK MOTOR CARS TO 1938 STOCK MOTOR CARS:

Orig. No.	Reno.	Date	Orig. No	Reno.	Date	Orig. No.	Reno.	Date
90324	**10324**	24.01.53	90331	**10331**	15.11.52	91328	**11328**	28.02.53
90325	**10325**	14.02.53	90332	**10332**	01.11.52	91329	**11329**	07.03.53
90326	**10326**	21.02.53	90333	**10333**	22.11.52	91330	**11330**	15.11.52
90327	**10327**	30.01.53	91324	**11324**	24.01.53	91331	**11331**	15.11.52
90328	**10328**	28.02.53	91325	**11325**	14.02.53	91332	**11332**	01.11.52
90329	**10329**	07.03.53	91326	**11326**	21.02.53	91333	**11333**	22.11.52
90330	**10330**	15.11.52	91327	**11327**	30.01.53			

CONVERSION OF NINE-CAR STOCK NDMs TO 1938 STOCK NDMs:

Orig. No.	Reno.	Date	Orig. No	Reno.	Date	Orig. No.	Reno.	Date
92029	12029	03.04.51	92039	12039	15.11.52	92049	12049	06.10.52
92030	12030	22.04.53	92040	12040	04.10.52	92050	12050	15.03.51
92031	12031	21.04.51	92041	12041	18.01.51	92051	12051	11.05.53
92032	12032	18.10.53	92042	12042	05.07.52	92052	12052	06.04.51
92033	12033	22.11.52	92043	12043	01.03.51	92053	12053	22.11.52
92034	12034	24.01.53	92044	12044	01.11.52	92054	12054	04.10.52
92035	12035	06.03.51	92045	12045	16.06.53	92056	12056	12.04.51
92036	12036	22.04.53	92046	12046	14.03.51	92057	12057	16.06.53
92037	12037	01.11.52	92047	12047	13.04.51			
92038	12038	01.11.52	92048	12048	22.04.53			

CONVERSION OF NINE-CAR STOCK NDMs TO 1938 STOCK 'A'-END UNDMs:

Orig. No.	Reno.	Date	Reno. to UNDM	Date	Orig. No.	Reno. to UNDM	Date
92055	12055	11.05.51	30000	23.06.52	92456	30011	05.07.52
92058			30001	28.10.52	92457	30012	23.09.51
92447			30002	15.11.51	92458	30013	12.11.52
92448			30003	09.10.52	92459	30014	15.11.51
92449			30004	14.01.53	92460	30015	17.04.52
92450			30005	05.11.52	92461	30016	12.06.51
92451			30006	02.10.51	92462	30017	08.08.52
92452			30007	06.06.52	92463	30018	13.03.53
92453			30008	23.01.53	92464	30019	19.05.52
92454			30009	30.09.52	92465	30020	29.08.51
92455			30010	06.03.53	92466	30021	18.12.52

CONVERSION OF NINE-CAR STOCK TRAILERS TO 1938 STOCK TRAILERS:

Orig. No.	Reno.	Date	Reno.	Date	Orig. No.	Reno.	Date	Reno.	Date
092389	A92389	22.02.44	012389	05.07.52	092399	A92399	19.02.44	012399	12.12.52
092390	A92390	22.02.44	012390	11.07.50	092400	A92400	26.02.44	012400	23.05.51
092391	A92391	26.02.44	012391	07.03.53	092401	A92401	25.03.44	012401	24.09.52
092392	A92392	19.02.44	012392	27.10.50	092402	A92402	11.03.44	012402	28.07.50
092393	A92393	29.01.44	012393	17.05.51	092403			012403	22.11.52
092394			012394	30.09.52	092404	A92404	18.03.44	012404	24.09.52
092395	A92395	22.04.44	012395	28.02.52	092405			012405	11.10.52
092396	A92396	05.02.44	012396	01.06.51	092406			012406	11.10.52
092397	A92397	25.03.44	012397	13.10.50	092407			012407	30.09.52
092398	A92398	01.04.44	012398	07.09.50	092408			012408	22.11.52

CHAPTER SIX

THE 1952 TUBE STOCK

The need for what became the 1952 Tube Stock came about as a consequence of the Second World War. The extensions to the Central Line required the trains of Pre-1938 Tube Stock which had been displaced by the new 1938 Tube Stock in 1938–41. For that purpose, the Pre-1938 cars passed through Acton Works for overhaul and equipment improvements but most had to be stored because work on the extensions had to be deferred. At the end of the war, work on the Central Line extensions resumed and opened in stages between 1946 and 1949. The trains for those extensions, however, had been stored for some six years and even though they again passed through Acton Works, being given a thorough rehabilitation, their reliability in service was not as good as had been anticipated. Furthermore, the Piccadilly Line was also in urgent need of additional trains, and plans to overcome both problems were formulated, beginning in 1948.

New rolling stock was therefore decided upon. London Transport were anxious to avoid the excessive teething problems it had gone through with the 1938 Tube Stock when new, which was made more painful because of wartime constraints. To that end, a number of experiments with train equipment and décor were undertaken, mostly on selected cars of the then still fairly new 1938 Tube Stock, so that when the new cars entered service, new ideas and technology would have already been proved.

Below The 1952 Tube Stock did not get beyond the planning and mock-up stage and the proposed design of driving motor car is seen in Acton Works. The finish was much more 'angular' than the 1938/49 stock, especially at the cab ends and at the beginning of the roof curve, but had curved bodywork below waist level. The circular and high car windows were taken from the experiment on 1938 Tube Stock DM 10306. *LT Museum*

Opposite Interior view of the 1952 Tube Stock. *LT Museum*

The simplest solution to both the Central and Piccadilly lines' problems was seen to be new rolling stock for the latter, which would include the additional trains required to boost the service. Therefore 100 seven-car trains were envisaged. Because the Central Line had the older Pre-1938 Tube Stock, the later batches from the Piccadilly Line (much of which had not been stored during the war) would be transferred to the Central Line. This would enable the older and more unreliable cars to be withdrawn, but at the same time, an increase of all train lengths on the main Central Line from seven to eight cars. This latter point was always an aspiration for the Central Line, for it was not achieved until many years later, and outside the period covered by this book.

One of the most noticeable features of the 1952 Tube Stock was to have been car windows curving up in line with the roof, including the windows in the sliding passenger doors. Two designs were produced, one being akin to the modifications made on 1938 Tube Stock DM 10306 in 1949. The passenger door windows curved in line with the roof as did the pair of windows in each bay. At the door pocket casements, circular windows were envisaged. The alternative design incorporated standard rectangular windows at the door pocket casements.

Whilst the proposed new 1952 Tube Stock was to have been an updated version of the 1938 Tube Stock, the body above floor level was to be constructed in aluminium, giving a weight saving per car of around 12%. Consideration was also being given to an unpainted finish but because trials with this on selected District Line 'R' stock cars were still at an early stage, no decision had been taken and the official drawings showed red-painted vehicles.

A mock-up of the proposed new stock was constructed at Acton Works, comprising the cab, leading saloon area and first pair of double doors. It incorporated the 'high saloon windows' and circular windows at the door pockets and adjacent to the cab. Inside, fluorescent lighting and fans were fitted. Whilst its relationship with the 1938 Tube Stock could clearly be seen and understood, it was unique and lacked its finesse in having 'sharp' rather than 'rounded' edges on the cab corners, cab windows and roof line. Passenger door control would also be fitted – a first for the Piccadilly Line.

Whilst the project had commenced in 1948, the British Transport Commission approved 'in principle' the new trains in 1950, with Metro-Cammell being awarded the contract for design. The project had drifted somewhat, however, which led to the stock being redesignated 1952 Tube Stock – it was originally known as the 1951 stock. The reasons for the delays were many and varied –

- Protracted discussions as to the final design.
- Tight financial constraints of post-war Britain.
- Energy and material shortages.
- Higher cost of constructing vehicles in aluminium.
- Additional costs with incorporating 'high windows'

In the light of the above, and because there had been a decrease in passenger numbers since 1948, London Transport decided in September 1952 not to proceed with new trains but would re-appraise the situation again in 1955. This it did (in 1954), but it was decided that the Pre-1938 Tube Stock on the Central Line could continue for another five years, or so, before being replaced.

CHAPTER SEVEN

THE 1956–59 TUBE STOCK

Prototype Trains

Long before the 1956 Prototype Tube Stock was conceived, there were plans for what became known as the 1951 (which later became 1952) Tube Stock. Destined for the Piccadilly Line, the proposed 100 new seven-car trains were to increase capacity on that line (a seven-car train of new stock with underfloor mounted equipment had greater passenger accommodation than a seven-car train of Pre-1938 Standard stock and also 40 trains per hour in the central area were envisaged), and the releasing of the newer cars of Pre-1938 stock, which the Piccadilly had, to the Central meant that the latter's capacity could also be increased, with all trains being formed of eight cars (which was intended anyway, but could not be achieved because of the unreliability of the Pre-1938 rehabilitated cars that had been stored, mostly in the open, during the war). The Piccadilly Line's displaced Pre-1938 stock would enable the oldest cars of that family (1923 vintage) on the Central to be withdrawn and scrapped. As has been described in the previous chapter, the 1952 stock was abandoned.

The Metro-Cammell-built train of 1956 Tube Stock poses on the Piccadilly Line test tracks near South Ealing. The body of this train was truly all unpainted aluminium, including the roof. Note the mechanical coupler which was fitted to outer end DMs. *LT Museum*

At the end of 1959, just two trains of 1959 Tube Stock had been delivered and one had entered service. Leading is DM 1012 of the first train, seen in Ruislip depot in December 1959 before being transferred to Northfields and entering service. Note the differences between this and the Prototype train, including the roof finished in light grey. *LT Museum*

A subsequent resurrection of the plan to replace the rolling stock on the Piccadilly Line led to three seven-car prototype trains being ordered by London Transport in 1954. The main features of these trains were aluminium bodies, rubber suspension of the bogies and wheels and fluorescent lighting. One seven-car train each was to be built by Metro-Cammell, Birmingham R.C.&W. Co., and the Gloucester R.C.&W. Co. Like the 1938 Tube Stock, each train would be formed of a three- and four-car unit. The publicity of the time suggested that the trains should be delivered 'in the spring of 1956', and it thus became known as the 1956 Prototype Tube Stock. Early drawings in the railway press showed an aluminium tube train with a waist-level red stripe, which was pointed downwards on the cab ends, as in R stock fashion. At that time also, it was suggested that the three trains would be operated on various tube lines '... to enable full operating and maintenance experience to be gained before it is necessary to place large-scale production orders'. In the event, they were operated only on the Piccadilly Line, which was to become the recipient of the production batch of stock, the 1959 Tube Stock, of which more in a moment. Other innovations to be introduced on the 1956 stock included improved mercury retarders and e.p. braking system, retractable shoegear, key-resetting passenger emergency handles (enabling easier identification of misuse), rubber surrounds to the windows, flat instead of grooved door runners and outside door indicator lights. Inside the cars, fluorescent lighting was to be used for the first time in tube stock, but at that time it was not considered possible to fit it in the traditional position and thus pairs of fluorescent tubes were fitted along the centre of the ceilings of the cars running from one end to the other. This followed a trial on 1938 stock DM 11294 on the Northern Line from November 1953 until January 1959. A re-arrangement of the transverse seating bays in the centre section of the saloon was also undertaken, to provide two sets of facing pairs on each side of the centre aisle. The blue interior paint scheme subsequently adopted came as a result of trials of this colour in 1938 stock cars 12006 and 11024 running on the Piccadilly Line from October 1955. Tip-up seats at the trailing ends of all cars were abolished, except for one (key operated and locked away when not in use) at each guard's gangway position.

Although the inner (middle) driving motor cars had fully automatic Wedgelock couplers, the outer driving motor cars had only a simple mechanical coupler. Formed into three- and four-car units, the car numbering system appeared to be following the number sequence of the time, being in the 4xxxx series (the District Line's R stock was numbered 2xxxx, the 1949 stock UNDMs were 3xxxx). The trains were formed up as follows:

	DM	T	NDM	DM	DM	T	DM
Metro-Cammell:	40000–45000–44000–43000 + 42000–45001–41000						
Birmingham:	40001–45002–44001–43001 + 42001–45003–41001						
Gloucester:	40002–45004–44002–43002 + 42002–45005–41002						

As with any new rolling stock, there is usually an element of slippage in actual completion and delivery. The first unit to arrive was not until 21 June 1957, which was a three-car unit from Metro-Cammell. Four cars from Gloucester came next on 12 July followed by the four-car unit from Metro-Cammell on 23 July. The three outstanding Gloucester cars arrived on 8 August, leaving the train built by Birmingham still outstanding. This duly arrived, the three-car unit on 4 December 1957 and the four-car unit on 7 January 1958

The first (Metro-Cammell) train entered public service on the Piccadilly Line on 9 September 1957, followed by the Gloucester train a month later on 7 October. The Birmingham train did not enter service until 14 April 1958. Within the three trains, each were operationally compatible. When still new, the Metro-Cammell train worked some non-stop special trips on Mondays to Fridays between the peaks between Acton Town and Hounslow West on Mondays to Fridays from 1 to 10 January 1958 as a public relations exercise, for the price of 1/– [5p] (adult) and 6d [2½p] (child) per round trip.

The three trains were very similar in appearance to each other, but there were minor differences. As the Metro-Cammell design was eventually adopted for the main order, the external visible differences between that and the other two can be summarised as follows: Both the Birmingham and the Gloucester trains did not have the upswept cantrail 'line' on the front cab ends over the front cab door. The 'roof' line thus started higher almost at roof level. The pair of ventilators on the Gloucester train had thin surrounding aluminium frames, while those on the Birmingham were flush with bodywork. The roof line of the Birmingham train had a thin aluminium beading line and was very slightly more rounded, while that of the Gloucester was slightly more angular at a slightly lower level. The Birmingham train followed the Metro-Cammell pattern in having flush side panels and curved rain strips over the doors, while the Gloucester train had a beading line in aluminium at waist level and straight rain strips over the doors, tapering downwards at the ends. Otherwise the 1956 stock was really an updated version of the 1938/49 Tube Stock and included the feature of having deep seat cushions, which the production cars did not have.

Being non-standard and incompatible with the rest of the Piccadilly Line fleet, these trains had specific workings in the timetable. At that time uncoupling was still in operation on the Piccadilly Line and these trains were also uncoupled in off-peak service and on Sundays. With a four-car unit following a three-car unit, the three-car uncoupled unit assumed a set number in the 2xx series. It is interesting to recall that this was the first instance of three-car passenger train

operation on the Piccadilly Line since the 1930s, but the 1956 stock three-car unit trailer cars had two compressors, which for many years had been the minimum requirement for any train formation on the main running line.

Production Trains – The 1959 Tube Stock

Sufficient experience had been gained with the prototype trains for, later in 1958, an order to be placed with Metro-Cammell for the replacement of the Pre-1938 Tube Stock on the Piccadilly Line. This order in fact comprised 76 seven-car trains, and together with the three prototype trains and the 15 trains of 1938/49 stock, would make up the total stock (94 trains) required for that line.

The 76 trains of what became known as the 1959 Tube Stock were to cost (at 1958 prices), £10,120,000 – or just over £133,000 per train. It was then envisaged that deliveries would be between the autumn of 1959 and mid-1962. This was largely adhered to, although changes of plan early into the delivery programme caused different delivery patterns. This is, however, outside the scope of this work.

In addition to Metro-Cammell providing the bodies and bogies, other equipment was provided as follows:

- Traction control & auxiliary equipment – British Thomson Houston.
- Braking equipment – Westinghouse.
- Motor generators – Metropolitan-Vickers.
- Door equipment – G.D. Peters.
- Automatic couplers – A.E.C.
- Roller bearing axleboxes & suspension bearings – Hoffman.
- Bolster and axlebox suspension – Metalastik.

Similar in most respects to the three prototype trains, the first seven-car train of 1959 stock arrived at Ruislip depot on 1 December 1959. After commissioning it was transferred to Northfields on 12 December and entered passenger service just two days later. Three instantly recognisable differences were (1) the twin marker lights instead of the five-headlight code arrangement, (2) the abandonment of the deep-cushion seating, and (3) a different but more logical system of car numbering. Gaps were left at the beginning of the 1959 Tube Stock numbering series to accommodate the 1956 stock at a later date.

Although the train formations were the same as their 1956 stock counterparts (M-T-NDM-M+M-T-M) and with each trailer having two compressors, the 1959 stock did not operate short trains in service. By the time of the first train entering service, uncoupling had been cancelled for the 1959 Christmas shopping traffic build-up – it was never reinstated. By the end of 1959, two seven-car trains had been delivered and one was in passenger service.

The initial order of 1959 Tube Stock actually placed with Metro-Cammell was as follows:

Driving motor cars	304	(numbered 1012–1315)
Trailers	152	(even numbers only 2012–2314)
Non-driving motor cars	76	(alternate odd numbers only 9013–9313)

Opposite Interior of a 1959 Tube Stock driving motor car when new, looking towards the trailing (guard's) end. Compared with the 1938 Tube Stock, the transverse seats on the new trains had been re-arranged in facing pairs. The 1959 stock seats lacked the deep cushions that were provided on the 1956 prototype trains. *LT Museum*

1956 PROTOTYPE TUBE STOCK DRIVING MOTOR CARS – 12

Deliv.	Entered service	Line	No.	Built
23.07.57	09.09.57	P	**40000**	MCW
07.01.58	14.04.58	P	**40001**	BRCW
08.08.57	07.10.57	P	**40002**	GRCW
21.06.57	09.09.57	P	**41000**	MCW
04.12.57	14.04.58	P	**41001**	BRCW
12.07.57	07.10.57	P	**41002**	GRCW
21.06.57	09.09.57	P	**42000**	MCW
04.12.57	14.04.58	P	**42001**	BRCW
12.07.57	07.10.57	P	**42002**	GRCW
23.07.57	09.09.57	P	**43000**	MCW
07.01.58	14.04.58	P	**43001**	BRCW
12.07.57	07.10.57	P	**43002**	GRCW

1956 PROTOTYPE TUBE STOCK TRAILERS – 6

Deliv.	Entered service	Line	No.	Built
23.07.57	09.09.57	P	**45000**	MCW
21.06.57	09.09.57	P	**45001**	MCW
07.01.58	14.04.58	P	**45002**	BRCW
04.12.57	14.04.58	P	**45003**	BRCW
12.07.57	07.10.57	P	**45004**	GRCW
08.08.57	07.10.57	P	**45005**	GRCW

1956 PROTOTYPE TUBE STOCK NON-DRIVING MOTOR CARS – 3

Deliv.	Entered service	Line	No.	Built
23.07.57	09.09.57	P	**44000**	MCW
07.01.58	14.04.58	P	**44001**	BRCW
12.07.57	07.10.57	P	**44002**	GRCW

1959 TUBE STOCK DRIVING MOTOR CARS – 8 (304)

Deliv.	Entered service	Line	No.	Deliv.	Entered service	Line	No.
01.12.59	14.12.59	P	**1012**	15.12.59	—	P	**1016**
01.12.59	14.12.59	P	**1013**	15.12.59	—	P	**1017**
01.12.59	14.12.59	P	**1014**	15.12.59	—	P	**1018**
01.12.59	14.12.59	P	**1015**	15.12.59	—	P	**1019**

1959 TUBE STOCK TRAILERS – 4 (152)

Deliv.	Entered service	Line	No.	Deliv.	Entered service	Line	No.
01.12.59	14.12.59	P	**2012**	15.12.59	—	P	**2016**
01.12.59	14.12.59	P	**2014**	15.12.59	—	P	**2018**

1959 TUBE STOCK NON-DRIVING MOTOR CARS – 2 (76)

Deliv.	Entered service	Line	No.	Deliv.	Entered service	Line	No.
01.12.59	14.12.59	P	**9013**	15.12.59	—	P	**9017**